The Fourth Battle of Winchester

The Fourth Battle

of Winchester

Toward a New Civil War Paradigm

Richard M. McMurry

The Kent State University Press ▣ Kent & London

© 2002 by The Kent State University Press, Kent, Ohio 44242
Library of Congress Card Catalog Number 2001002197
ISBN 0-87338-721-X
Manufactured in the United States of America

06   05   04   03   02   5   4   3   2   1

Library of Congress Cataloging-in-Publication Data

McMurry, Richard M.
The Fourth Battle of Winchester : toward a new Civil War paradigm /
Richard M. McMurry.
p.   cm.
Includes Index.
ISBN 0-87338-721-X (pbk. : alk. paper)
1. Virginia—History—Civil War, 1861–1865—Campaigns.
2. Winchester (Va.)—History, Military—19th Century.
3. Shenandoah River Valley (Va. and W. Va.)—History—
Civil War, 1861–1865—Campaigns.
4. United States—History—Civil War, 1861–1865—Campaigns.
5. United States—History—Civil War, 1861–1865—Historiography.
6. Counterfactuals (Logic).
I. Title

E476.5 .M38   2002
973.7'3—dc21   2001002197

British Cataloging-in-Publication data are available.

For two great friends who made life a whole lot better—
Cecil and Sparkplug

No historian is ever wholly content merely with establishing (in so far as he can establish) *what* happened in history; he must go on and ask *why* it happened. It is this *why* that has fascinated historians from the beginning of time, and that gives excitement and meaning to historical inquiry.

HENRY STEELE COMMAGER

Someone has to propose ideas at the boundaries of the plausible in order to so annoy the experimentalists and observationalists that they'll be motivated to disprove the idea.

CARL SAGAN

History is supposed to be fun.

ARNOLD SHANKMAN

Contents

Acknowledgments

At its best the study of the American Civil War in general and of its military side in particular is a collective enterprise undertaken by friends who have a common interest in the great struggle and who gleefully share ideas and new information about the people and events of the 1860s. Over the years many such friends from all over the country and, indeed, the world have contributed to this book, most of them indirectly by the comments about the war—and often about other subjects as well—that they have made from time to time. Some of them may recognize parts of this work as having grown from remarks they made at this or that gathering or in one or more of their publications. Many of these ideas, however, originated in conversations and arguments and were tossed about under such circumstances and conditions of insobriety that it is not now possible to ascertain who first came up with the suggestion. To all such fellow "Civil Warriors," I owe much.

Seven friends were kind enough to read and critique this manuscript. Larry Daniel, Jack Davis, Gary Gallagher, Joe Glatthaar, John Hubbell, Bob Krick, and Steve Woodworth, distinguished historians all, kindly took time from their busy schedules to read an earlier version of the work, and it has benefited greatly from their efforts and suggestions. They, of course, are not responsible for any errors of fact that may remain or for my interpretations.

Joe and Steve, it must be said, do not share fully my great admiration for George H. Thomas and doubtless will welcome this complete exoneration from any complicity in the statements about him that appear in the text. Bob, as all of his many friends know, disagrees with many—

perhaps most—of the arguments put forth in these pages. Good fellow that he is, he nevertheless slogged through the essay at considerable risk to his health (blood pressure), and his numerous and valuable suggestions have helped greatly improve whatever quality of style the text possesses. His corrections of several errors of fact and his questioning of many of my assertions led me to correct, revise, or restate many of them and, I hope, to strengthen my thesis.

To my son Jonathan go my usual thanks for help with the accursed machine that spends its days sitting on my desk, plotting to make my life miserable. Jonathan also read the work in an earlier version and made many valuable suggestions.

A note on the notes: Since this work contains no formal bibliography, I have included complete information about each source in the note where it is first cited. Normally, I avoid this pedantry since such information usually duplicates the bibliography, burdens the reader, wastes space and paper, and in general serves no useful purpose.

The nature of this study—counterfactual history, actual history, and a discussion of the work of other historians—necessitated including much information that is, in effect, a debate with the work of other writers. Most of this material is in the text in one form or another. On several occasions, however, I have elected to put discussions of relatively minor matters or examples in footnotes rather than to clutter the text and deflect readers from the main argument.

Preface

Those of us fortunate enough to spend our adult lives studying the history of the American Civil War often receive invitations to speak at seminars, symposia, Civil War round table meetings, and similar gatherings all across the country. Anyone who addresses more than a few such groups will quickly learn that hundreds of the people who participate in the question-and-answer sessions frequently delight in subjecting the speakers to veritable barrages of "counterfactual" questions.

These sometimes wacky queries revolve around this kind of question: "What would have happened if what did happen had not happened and 'X' had happened instead?" Almost any phrase containing one or more proper nouns and, perhaps, a verb or two can be inserted in place of the "X."

Of all the hundreds of counterfactual Civil War questions I have been asked over the past three decades, I have known the answers to only five:

1. What would have happened if Braxton Bragg had used an atomic bomb at Perryville?

He probably would have won a clear tactical victory for the Confederates, but you can never know. Being Braxton Bragg, he might have vaporized his own army, thereby effectively ending the war in mid-October 1862.

2. What would have happened if Ulysses S. Grant had commanded the Yankee army at Chancellorsville in May 1863?

Today those of us living in what are now the United States and Canada would be speaking German, and most of our histories of the American

Civil War, along with most of the other books as well as almost all of the magazines and newspapers published in Europe and North America, would be written in that language.

Had Grant been in Virginia in May 1863 to command the Union forces in the Battle of Chancellorsville, he and the Confederates under Gen. Robert E. Lee would have fought one or more titanic and bloody, but inconclusive, engagements similar to those they, in fact, fought across the Old Dominion a year later. Meanwhile, with Grant in Virginia, Maj. Gen. John A. McClernand, as the senior officer present, would have commanded the Union force then endeavoring to capture Vicksburg, Mississippi.

With McClernand in command of the Yankees in the Vicksburg area, the Rebels would have captured Chicago, Indianapolis, Columbus, Pittsburgh, Philadelphia, Baltimore, and Washington. Lt. Gen. John C. Pemberton, commander of the secessionist army defending Vicksburg, would have become the greatest hero of the Confederacy when he forced President Abraham Lincoln to acknowledge Southern independence in a White House ceremony in occupied Washington. After such a triumph, Pemberton—a native of Pennsylvania—would easily have won the 1867 election and become (on February 22, 1868) the second president of the Confederate States of America.

With the United States broken into at least two (and, quite probably, within a few years into four or five or more) weak, Balkan-like nations, Germany would have won the World War and imposed her rule on the Western world.[1] North America would have become just one more colonial possession of Imperial Germany, and German would have become our official language.

On the positive side, we should note that Pemberton's 1863 series of Confederate victories, the resulting independence of the Confederacy, and the consequent 1918 triumph of Kaiser Wilhelm's Germany would have meant that Adolph Hitler would happily have lived out his days in the Old Soldiers' Home in Landsberg, fifty miles west of Munich. There,

---

1. The 1914–18 conflagration would have been *the* World War because there would not have been a second such conflict.

we can imagine, he would have passed his time painting postcards and writing his reminiscences, *Mein Kampf*—a work that would have won highly favorable reviews when translated into English (a language still spoken in Australia, New Zealand, Tasmania, the Falkland Islands, and a few other isolated and far-flung fragments of the once-great British Empire) as *The Memoirs of a Bohemian Corporal in the Great War.* The motion picture, which almost certainly would have starred Charlie Chaplin, would also have received much critical acclaim.

3. What would have happened if Gen. Robert E. Lee and the Confederates had won the Battle of Gettysburg in July 1863?

Lee would have ridden up to the crest of Cemetery Ridge late on the blistering afternoon of July 3, passing through the human wreckage of the Rebel brigades that had made the great charge that broke the Yankee line. At the crest he would have been greeted by a few hundred of his victorious and wildly cheering soldiers standing amid the captured Federal cannon, waving their red battleflags in triumph. Off to the front and to his left and right, Lee would have observed scores of Union regiments, their sturdy ranks unbroken, calmly pulling back to the east to take up another strong defensive position on the next line of hills or behind the next creek.

Even as he savored his most recent tactical triumph, Lee would have realized that his was a pyrrhic victory. He had lost more than one-third of his army in the three days of fighting at Gettysburg, his men had begun to run short of ammunition, the food that they could collect from the surrounding farms would soon be exhausted, and he had no secure, dependable supply line to his base in Virginia. In addition, his army was burdened with several thousand prisoners and some twelve thousand wounded men. Once those facts sank in, Lee would have known that he had to get his battered troops back to Virginia.

Doubtless, the Confederate commander would have held his men at Gettysburg another day or two to bury the dead, gather up the wounded, and secure captured property. Those tasks completed—say, late on July 4—he would have withdrawn from the Gettysburg area and begun a slow march southward to the Potomac, where high water would have delayed the retreating secessionists for several days. The Rebels would not have been able to cross the river to reach safety in Virginia until about the middle of the month. Once back in the Old Dominion, Lee and his army would have had several weeks to rest, resupply, and prepare for the next campaign.

In a phrase, the result of a Confederate victory at Gettysburg would have been virtually indistinguishable from the actual event.

4. What would have happened if President Jefferson Davis had not removed Gen. Joseph E. Johnston from command of the Confederate army at Atlanta in mid-July 1864 and replaced him with Gen. John Bell Hood?

Atlanta would have fallen to the Federals three or four weeks sooner than it did, and the Confederacy would have come to its end two or three months before it in fact did so.

The fifth counterfactual Civil War question to which I know the answer is the subject of Parts 1, 2, and 3 of this essay.[2]

Counterfactual questions, if kept more or less within the parameters of what was possible at the time and place, can often help us better understand events of the past. In so doing, they can sometimes bring about a "paradigm shift"—a new way of thinking about history and hence of grasping its meaning. To the extent that such inquiries fulfill that purpose and lead us to a fuller appreciation of history, they can be legitimate and useful devices for the study of the past.

In the first three sections of this essay, I shall explore several ramifications of a counterfactual situation that, to say the least, strains the bound-

---

2. Another fascinating counterfactual Civil War assertion is to be found in a 1941 remark attributed to an elderly Rebel veteran. On December 8 of that year, a newspaper in an unnamed Southern city is supposed to have sent a reporter out to the local Confederate soldiers' home to interview the aged veterans as to what they thought of the events at Pearl Harbor on the previous day. One silver-haired old fellow reportedly drew himself erect and declared in a stentorian voice, "It never would have happened if Albert Sidney Johnston hadn't been killed at Shiloh!" I cannot vouch for the accuracy of the story, but the gentleman who told it to me is a lawyer, so it must be true.

ary between what was possible during the Civil War and what was not. Despite the high degree of implausibility (if not improbability, or even the outright impossibility) of the events narrated therein, I believe that a consideration of the counterfactual situation resulting from the events described in Parts 1, 2, and 3 below can greatly enhance our understanding of the military history of the Civil War in general and of the great campaigns of 1864 in particular. In Parts 4, 5, and 6, I shall turn what I consider the key lesson of the first three parts back to the actual events and historiographical accounts and in so doing attempt to show how what I believe to be the counterfactual truths of the first three parts can apply to the history of the Civil War and enhance our interpretations of it.

While the events described in the opening sections are fanciful, the underlying points, I believe, are valid. The counterfactual events, I hope, can help us see the points with greater clarity.[3]

---

3. Counterfactual history has become quite popular in recent years. See, for example, Alexander Demandt, *History That Never Happened: A Treatise on the Question What Would Have Happened If. . . .* (Jefferson, N.C.: McFarland, 1993); and Robert Cowley, ed., *What If? The World's Foremost Military Historians Imagine What Might Have Been* (New York: G. P. Putnam's, 1999). For a fictional, as opposed to counterfactual, treatment, see Harry Turtledove, *The Guns of the South* (New York: Ballantine, 1992).

For four fairly recent examples of a counterfactual approach to the study of the Civil War, see William C. Davis, "The Turning Point That Wasn't: The Confederates and the Election of 1864," in *The Cause Lost: Myths and Realities of the Confederacy* (Lawrence: Univ. Press of Kansas, 1996), 127–47; Peter G. Tsouras, *Gettysburg: An Alternate History* (Mechanicsburg, Pa.: Stackpole, 1997); Roger L. Ransom, "Fact and Counterfact: The 'Second American Revolution' Reconsidered," *Civil War History* 45 (1999): 28–60; and "Alternate History," *American Heritage* (Sept. 1999): 39–53, which consists of Phil Patton, "Lee Defeats Grant," 39–45; Fredric Smoler, "Past Tense," 45–49; and James M. McPherson, "Gettysburg 1862," 49–53.

Mackinlay Kantor's "History in Reverse: If the South Had Won the Civil War" (*Look* 24.24 [Nov. 22, 1960]: 29–62; published in book form the following year—New York: Bantam) is the classic counterfactual account of a victorious Confederacy. Kantor has the South winning at Gettysburg and Vicksburg in 1863. Maryland, Kentucky, and (eventually) Cuba then join the Confederacy, while Texas and the Indian Territory (Oklahoma) break off to form a third North American republic. The Rebels move their capital to the District of Dixie (formerly the District of Columbia); the rump Federal government transfers its capital to Columbia (formerly Columbus), Ohio. Afterward, the Confederacy abolishes slavery in 1885 during the administration of President James Longstreet. The Spanish-Confederate War is touched off when the battleship *Mississippi* explodes in Havana Harbor, and so forth. The three nations all fight Germany in World Wars I and II and happily reunite in late 1960.

The Fourth Battle of Winchester

PART ONE

The Fourth Battle
of Winchester

In the spring of 1864, at the beginning of the fourth year of the American Civil War, Lt. Gen. Ulysses S. Grant, recently promoted and placed in command of all Federal armies, planned to launch a five-pronged assault against the Confederacy. Grant hoped that by engaging the Rebels simultaneously on so many fronts and maintaining constant, unrelenting pressure against the secessionists on all of them, he would stretch Confederate manpower and resources to the breaking point; achieve success somewhere; and, by converting that success into a great victory, bring about the collapse of the rebellion.

Two of Grant's proposed assaults on Rebeldom could be described as major operations; three as relatively minor undertakings. Since any one of the five that achieved success could be exploited to bring about final victory, it really did not matter where the success came. Each of the five campaigns had the potential to become the decisive operation that snuffed out the South's bid for independence. Conversely, the Confederacy had to win—or at least to avoid defeat—everywhere to preserve its hope for nationhood. For the Rebels, to lose anywhere in 1864 would be to lose all.

One of the minor Union operations, commanded by Maj. Gen. Benjamin F. Butler, was to be launched up the James River in southeastern Virginia against the Richmond-Petersburg area. A second, under Maj. Gen. Franz Sigel, involved a thrust into the northern Shenandoah Valley in western Virginia. Maj. Gen. Nathaniel P. Banks was to lead the third minor operation, moving eastward from New Orleans (occupied by Northern forces in April 1862) against Mobile, Alabama, the Confederacy's last important port on the Gulf of Mexico.

The major efforts were to take place in east-central Virginia and in North Georgia. In the former operation, Grant himself would direct the Army of the Potomac as it moved against the Army of Northern Virginia commanded by Gen. Robert E. Lee. (Technically, Maj. Gen. George G. Meade commanded the Army of the Potomac, but Grant would be present with it, control its operations, and issue—through Meade—the orders for its movements.) Grant entrusted the Federal forces invading North Georgia to his good friend and favorite subordinate Maj. Gen. William T. Sherman.

Each of the three lesser campaigns quickly met with failure as the Southerners won convincing victories over Banks along the Red River in Louisiana, over Butler at Bermuda Hundred along the James River below Richmond, and over Sigel at New Market in the Shenandoah Valley. By mid-May, Grant's great five-pronged offensive had been reduced to the operations directed by himself and Sherman.

After a long, bloody summer, Sherman finally won the major victory that the Federal cause needed when he forced the Rebels to evacuate Atlanta, Georgia, during the night of September 1–2. Sherman's triumph touched off massive rejoicing by unionists everywhere and appeared to be the great success that would soon result in the reelection of President Abraham Lincoln, a complete national triumph, an end to the war, the abolition of slavery, and the restoration of the Union.

While Sherman and his troops maneuvered and fought their way across North Georgia to capture Atlanta, Grant and the Yankees in Virginia experienced a quite different fate in their great struggle against Lee. Through May and June the two armies clashed in a series of titanic battles in the Wilderness, at Spotsylvania Court House, on the North Anna River, at Cold Harbor, and along the lines of massive fortifications that quickly sprouted from the ground in front of Richmond and Petersburg.

Through mid-June, when Grant reeled back in defeat from his first assaults on the Petersburg trenches, he had lost a total of about 65,000 men. His army—its offensive capability greatly weakened, if not destroyed—found itself bogged down before the very strong Confederate earthworks protecting the Rebel capital and Petersburg. Lee, in fact, felt so secure in his great fortifications that in mid-June he detached a large part of his army under his most capable subordinate, Lt. Gen. Jubal A. Early, and sent it west to defend Lynchburg, where a new Union force had appeared.

Lee hoped that Early and his troops could drive away the unionists who menaced Lynchburg. They could then clear the area of all remaining Yankee forces, enter the Shenandoah Valley, secure the region's rich summer crops for the Southerners, alarm and demoralize the people of the North, and perhaps even compel Grant to detach troops from his army before Richmond and Petersburg and send them off to the Valley after Early. Such detachments would weaken the Union forces facing Lee. It was the old strategy that the Rebels had used to such good effect in 1862 in similar circumstances.

At first, Early's success exceeded all of Lee's expectations. Early and his troops quickly disposed of the Federal forces still in the Valley, marched north, swept across the Potomac River into Maryland, defeated a hastily gathered Northern army on July 9 in the Battle of the Monocacy, and for a few days menaced Washington, D.C. Even President Abraham Lincoln himself briefly came under fire from a few of Early's men when he paid a visit to some of the capital's fortifications.

Finding the works that protected the Federal capital too strong to assault, Early soon withdrew to the northern Shenandoah Valley. There he and his army remained—an annoying threat to the North and an embarrassing and irritating thorn in the Yankees' side. On July 24 Early routed a pursuing Union force in the Second Battle of Kernstown. A week later, to add insult to injury, some of his cavalry burned Chambersburg, Pennsylvania.

During August, in a belated effort to deal with the enormous military and political problems stemming from Early's presence in the lower Shenandoah Valley, Grant and Federal authorities created the "Middle Military Division" and placed it under the command of Maj. Gen. Philip H. Sheridan, formerly head of the cavalry forces in the army with Grant.[1]

1. The boundaries of Sheridan's new command are delineated in Frank J. Welcher, *The Union Army, 1861–1865: Organization and Operations,* vol. 1, *The Eastern Theater* (Bloomington: Indiana Univ. Press, 1989) 7–8; see also 293–94.

Sheridan's force totaled about 48,000 troops. His most important units were the Sixth Corps, under Maj. Gen. Horatio G. Wright, sent from Grant's lines in front of Richmond; two divisions of the Nineteenth Corps commanded by Maj. Gen. William H. Emory that had been in Louisiana until brought east and sent to the Shenandoah Valley; and some of the Union forces that had been operating in the western Virginia–West Virginia area (the Army of West Virginia, sometimes designated the Eighth Corps) under Brig. Gen. George Crook. Sheridan's field command—the Army of the Shenandoah—also included a three-division cavalry corps, commanded by Brig. Gen. Alfred T. A. Torbert.

As the strength of Sheridan's army increased, Lee raised the stakes in the Shenandoah Valley, dispatching reinforcements to Early from the Rebel lines at Richmond and Petersburg. These additions to Early's Army of the Valley brought Confederate strength in the area up to about 18,000 men.

Sheridan and Federal authorities, however, believed that Early commanded perhaps twice that number of troops. For that reason, and also because Northern officials did not want to chance a large-scale defeat with the crucial fall elections looming in October and November, Sheridan received instructions not to risk another setback. For five weeks, therefore, no serious fighting took place in the Valley. Sheridan and Early limited themselves to cautious actions, sparring occasionally with each other, but neither general willing to bring on a major engagement.[2]

In mid-September, Lee called some of Early's men back to the lines at Richmond. When Rebecca Wright, a Quaker schoolteacher in Winchester who doubled as a Union agent, sent word to Sheridan that troops had left Early's army, the Federal commander concluded that the time had come to strike.

Early—perhaps lulled into overconfidence by his foe's recent inactivity—had foolishly scattered his army. On September 19, in the Third

2. For background, see Jeffry D. Wert, *From Winchester to Cedar Creek: The Shenandoah Campaign of 1864* (Carlisle, Pa.: South Mountain Press, 1987), 1–41; Richard R. Duncan, *Lee's Endangered Left: The Civil War in Western Virginia, Spring of 1864* (Baton Rouge: Louisiana State Univ. Press, 1998); and Thomas A. Lewis, *The Shenandoah in Flames: The Valley Campaign of 1864* (New York: Time-Life Books, 1987).

Battle of Winchester, Sheridan pounced upon, overpowered, and routed the outnumbered Confederates. Three days later Sheridan's troops caught up with Early's men at Fisher's Hill some twenty miles south of Winchester and administered a second sound drubbing to the Rebels. Indeed, only some very bad generalship on the part of Sheridan's cavalry commander allowed the Southerners to escape from Fisher's Hill and continue their flight southward.[3]

After this great victory Sheridan pushed south up the Valley to Harrisonburg. Then, concluding that he had finally disposed of the pesky Early, the Yankee commander began to shift his troops back toward Winchester in the lower Valley, laying waste to the countryside as he went so that, he hoped, the area could not again provide sustenance for a Confederate army. Because he reasoned that no more serious fighting would occur in the Shenandoah Valley, Sheridan thought the time had come to return most of the Army of the Shenandoah to Grant's main force for the continuing operations against Richmond and Petersburg.[4]

Early and the Army of the Valley, however, were far from finished. After the debacle at Fisher's Hill, Lee returned to Early the troops whose departure had triggered Sheridan's September offensive. As Sheridan pulled his force back to the north, the crafty Rebel commander followed at a distance with his reinforced army.

On October 9 Early's cavalry, which had gotten too far ahead of its infantry support, ran into a large force of Federal horsemen at Tom's Brook near Fisher's Hill. The Yankees chased the Rebel cavalrymen back up the Valley for more than twenty miles (an episode known as the "Woodstock Races" in the annals of Sheridan's mounted force). The bulk of the Union army, however, continued its slow march northward. Early followed.

By October 13 Sheridan had his unionists in camp north of Cedar Creek and south of Middletown. Early's Confederates—infantry included

3. Wert, *Winchester to Cedar Creek*, 46–134.

4. Ibid., 142–45, 157–60, 165–66; John L. Heatwole, *The Burning: Sheridan in the Shenandoah Valley* (Charlottesville, Va.: Howell Press, 1998).

now—lurked only a mile or so to the south. Skirmishing over the next several days revealed to the Yankees the presence of a fairly large Southern force. Soon, however, Early pulled back southward to the Fisher's Hill area. Sheridan still thought that the Rebels in the Valley constituted no serious threat to his command.

Meanwhile, a disagreement had arisen between Sheridan and his superiors over the future employment of the Army of the Shenandoah. The Federal authorities summoned "Little Phil" to Washington to confer about the matter. Firmly convinced that the soundly whipped Early would remain passive, Sheridan departed for the national capital late on October 15. Maj. Gen. Horatio G. Wright assumed acting command of the army; Brig. Gen. James B. Ricketts ascended temporarily to the head of the Sixth Corps.[5]

When Sheridan departed for Washington, he left his army camped in the wide angle formed by the North Fork of the Shenandoah River on the east and Cedar Creek to the south and west. The creek flows generally from northwest to southeast and joins the river, which along that stretch flows from southwest to northeast.

The macadamized Valley Pike ran west of the river from Fisher's Hill north through Strasburg and then crossed Cedar Creek a mile or so above (west of) that stream's junction with the river. At the point where it crossed the creek, the pike ran from southwest to northeast, but a short distance north of the creek, the road bent to the north and ran on to Middletown, whence it continued northward down the Valley.

Along its lower stretches, Cedar Creek was about thirty yards wide and flowed between steep banks. Several fords on the lower section of the creek and others along the river near the creek's mouth offered points at which to cross those streams; Middletown lay about two miles from the point where the pike crossed the creek. Meadow Brook ran from north to south to the west of and parallel to the pike to join Cedar Creek about three-fourths of a mile above the point where the pike crossed the creek.

5. Wert, *Winchester to Cedar Creek,* 160–72.

Sheridan had posted most of his cavalry on the far right (west) of his position, and he stationed the Sixth Corps between the cavalry and Meadow Brook. In the highly unlikely event that Early dared initiate aggressive action, Sheridan assumed that the Rebel effort would come from the more open area to the west. For that reason, he posted the Sixth Corps, his best and most experienced unit, where it could most easily meet such an assault. The Nineteenth Corps and the Army of West Virginia held the ground from Meadow Brook eastward toward the river. Ridges that ran across the whole area separated the Federal camps and would make it difficult for the various units to support each other in the event of battle.[6]

On the afternoon of October 17, some of Early's subordinate commanders along with his topographical engineer Jedediah Hotchkiss climbed to the northern end of Three Top (or Massanutten) Mountain, from which they could examine Sheridan's position north of Cedar Creek. (Arthritis kept Early himself from making the trek.) From their lofty observatory, Maj. Gen. John B. Gordon, Hotchkiss, and the others studied the Yankee camps spread out on the far side of the river. The Rebel observers soon saw that the left (eastern) flank of the Union position was vulnerable to attack and realized that Sheridan had presented the Confederates with a golden opportunity to strike a blow that might reverse the tide that had been running against them in the Valley since mid-September. The Southern officers could scarcely contain their glee as they made their way back down the mountain.[7]

Early, an often gruff man who sometimes had great difficulty listening to his subordinates and accepting suggestions from them, proved surprisingly receptive to the proposal brought to him by Gordon, Hotchkiss, and the others. At a long conference on the following day, he and his chief lieutenants hammered out the details of their plan. Gordon, with

6. Ibid., 170–71.

7. Jedediah Hotchkiss, *Make Me a Map of the Valley: The Civil War Journal of Stonewall Jackson's Topographer*, ed. Archie P. McDonald (Dallas: Southern Methodist Univ. Press, 1973), 237–38; John B. Gordon, *Reminiscences of the Civil War* (1903; reprint, Dayton, Ohio: Morningside, 1985), 333–35.

the bulk of Early's little army, would make a night march, cross the river, follow a "pig's path" along the northern nose of the mountain, cross back to the left bank of the river below (north of) its junction with Cedar Creek, deploy, and at 5:00 A.M. on the nineteenth launch an assault against the weak eastern side of the Yankee position.

At the same time, most of the remaining units of the small Confederate army, the most important of which was the infantry division of Maj. Gen. Joseph B. Kershaw, would cross Cedar Creek near the Valley Pike and assail the Federals from the south. Rebel cavalry would be on either flank of the attacking force.

Early entrusted what turned out to be the key part of his battle plan to the small infantry division (three Virginia brigades) of Brig. Gen. Gabriel C. Wharton. While Gordon and Kershaw attacked the Yankees from the east and south, Wharton's three brigades, followed by a battalion of artillery, were to march northward along the Valley Pike, passing behind the attacking units as they pushed the enemy off to the west, and seize the road at and north of Middletown. Since the pike there commanded the ground to the west and south, control of the road at Middletown would give the Confederates mastery of the battlefield.

Early was an unusually audacious general and a staunch advocate of aggressive warfare, but his Cedar Creek plan was daring even by his standards. Jeffry Wert, one historian of the 1864 Shenandoah Valley Campaign, called it "a brilliantly conceived gamble unparalleled during the war."[8]

When the Rebels struck on the morning of the nineteenth, they achieved a complete surprise—"the most impressive surprise attack of the war," in the words of historian Gary W. Gallagher. Within little more than half an hour, the unionists south of Middletown and east of Meadow Brook had been routed—driven "in wild confusion," noted engineer Hotchkiss in his diary entry for that day.[9]

8. Wert, *Winchester to Cedar Creek,* 24, 175; Gordon, *Reminiscences,* 335–37.

9. Gallagher, *Lee and His Generals in War and Memory* (Baton Rouge: Louisiana State Univ. Press, 1998), 191; Hotchkiss, *Make Me a Map,* 239.

Ahead of the onrushing Rebels, thousands of frightened Northern soldiers fled westward toward Meadow Brook, desperate to find shelter behind the Sixth Corps. Hundreds of other Yankees fell into the hands of the pursuing Confederates. Among their captives the Southerners counted Col. Rutherford B. Hayes, commanding a brigade in the Army of West Virginia, and Capt. William McKinley of the 23d Ohio Infantry Regiment. The two Northern officers thus became the third and fourth future U.S. presidents to spend time as prisoners of war (George Washington and Andrew Jackson were the others).

By 8:00 A.M. the Confederates had overrun much of the Union position, and the Third Division of the Sixth Corps, commanded by Brig. Gen. George Washington Getty, was the only organized significant Union infantry force remaining on the field. Realizing the precarious situation he then faced, Getty grimly prepared for the great attack that he knew would soon fall upon his division. For his heroic stand on that nineteenth of October, he would win the immortal sobriquet "the Rock of Cedar Creek."

As Getty and his veterans steeled themselves for the next great Confederate onslaught, Sheridan, en route back to the army from the conference in Washington, heard the sounds of the battle and galloped southward from Winchester "twenty miles away" (as a poet later put it, increasing the actual distance by about eight miles). As he neared the battlefield, Sheridan found himself caught up in a panicked mass of fleeing men, wagons, horses, mules, and cannon. Deaf to Sheridan's loud, furious, profane, and blasphemous pleas to rally and make a stand, the stricken soldiers continued their headlong flight, carrying their angry, cursing commander, mounted on his great black horse Rienzi, along with them.

At about the time Sheridan was being swept off the field and back toward Winchester, two Confederate divisions—those of Maj. Gen. Stephen Dodson Ramseur and Brig. Gen. John Pegram—began a costly and, as it turned out, unsuccessful attack on Getty's position. Conferring after their repulse, Ramseur and Pegram concluded that Wharton's Division, then marching northward along the pike in conformity with Early's plan, should be diverted from its original mission and utilized as part of a second assault on Getty.[10]

Soon encountering Early, Ramseur and Pegram explained the situation and urged their proposal on the Rebel commander. Following a brief discussion, Early yielded to his subordinates' pleas and was about to issue the necessary orders when Gordon rode up to join the group. After congratulating Gordon on the success of his attack, Early explained the situation and the change of plan. While the Confederate generals talked, a grimy Yankee gunner of Battery E, 5th Maine Artillery, posted on a ridge about one-half mile to the west, spotted the group of secessionist horsemen, guessed that it was a gathering of important officers, carefully aimed his 20-pounder Parrott gun, and yanked the lanyard.

Gordon had just acquiesced in the change of plan when a shell exploded almost directly above the little group of generals. It was to go down in the records as one of the most accurate artillery shots of the war. It was also the only time in the conflict that one projectile put four general officers out of action. Ironically, however, it was the shot that was to do more to help the Confederate cause than any other fired in the Old Dominion during the war, except for those that struck Gen. Joseph E. Johnston on May 31, 1862, at Seven Pines, knocking him out of the command of the Confederate army in Virginia and leading to the naming of Robert E. Lee as his replacement.[11]

A shell fragment struck Early in the back of his head, and the irascible lieutenant general died before his feet slipped from the stirrups. Pegram and Gordon were so stunned by the concussion that they were rendered unconscious, and members of their staffs soon moved them to a nearby field hospital. Ramseur was badly—and, as it turned out,

10. In the Confederate army, brigades, divisions, and corps were designated by the name of their commander. Thus, "Wharton's Division" (but not "Gabriel C. Wharton's division") is a proper noun and is capitalized accordingly. Such units in the Union army were designated by number and, therefore, "Getty's division" is not a proper noun.

11. "The shot that struck me down was the best ever fired for the Southern Confederacy, for I possessed in no degree the confidence of the Government, and now a man who does enjoy it will succeed me," declared Johnston after his wound. See Dabney H. Maury, "Interesting Reminiscences of General Johnston," *Southern Historical Society Papers* 18 (1890): 181; and *Recollections of a Virginian in the Mexican, Indian, and Civil Wars* (New York: Charles Scribner's Sons, 1894), 151.

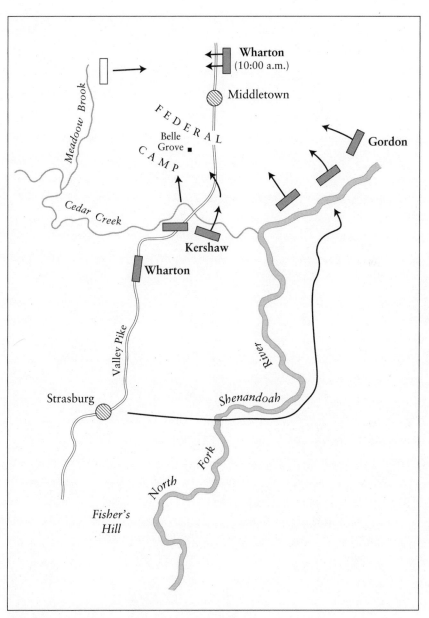

The Battle of Cedar Creek, as narrated in the text.

mortally—wounded by a shell fragment that struck him in the side. Aides did what they could for the dying general on the spot and quickly carried him off to the nearby Belle Grove Plantation house where he succumbed to his wounds the following morning, his last hours made a bit easier by the company of two of his old friends, George A. Custer and Wesley Merritt—Federal brigadier generals, then prisoners of war.

Even as horrified staff officers and aides hastened forward to attend the wounded Rebel generals, a courier galloped southward to find Kershaw and notify him that he had just become commander of the Army of the Valley. With Early, Gordon, Ramseur, and Pegram all removed from the scene, nobody knew of the change of plan on which they had agreed.

More than half an hour passed after Early's death before Kershaw learned of his elevation to overall command of the secessionist forces and longer still before he could make his way to the northern part of the battlefield to familiarize himself with the situation there. Meanwhile, Wharton, ignorant of the change of plan and acting under the orders he had received the night before, kept his men trudging northward along the pike.

Sometime soon after 9 o'clock that morning, Wharton secured possession of the pike at and north of Middletown and found that he had completely outflanked the Union position to the southwest. A battalion of Rebel artillery commanded by Col. Thomas H. Carter galloped down the pike to join Wharton's infantry. Within a few minutes of their arrival, Carter's guns began to pound the Yankees off to their left-front. A heroic charge by Federal horsemen who rushed across the field from their original post on the far western side of the Union position encountered blasts of infantry and artillery fire that left the open space west of the pike covered with a bloody mass of dead and wounded men and horses.

It was too much. Even Getty's sturdy Sixth Corps veterans could stand it no longer. Realizing that Confederate possession of the pike at Middletown made it impossible for the Yankees to remain on the field, Getty reluctantly gave the order for all Federal troops still involved in the fight to pull back to the west—the only safe direction of retreat that remained open to them. Getty hoped that he would be able to swing around to the north to reach Winchester, where he expected to find Brig. Gen. John Ricketts, commanding the Sixth Corps, or perhaps Wright and Sheridan themselves.

By 11:00 or 11:30 A.M. the Confederates had completed their triumph at Cedar Creek. Never in the Civil War—and rarely in any war—had so outnumbered a field army won so overwhelming a victory over so strong a foe in so short a time. Even more remarkable, the Rebels had won their complete success while fighting on the tactical offensive during a war in which the army standing on the defensive usually enjoyed great battlefield advantages.

Kershaw, however, saw immediately that the battlefield victory, as complete as it was, could be the opening to an even greater success for the Southerners. Quickly, as the last of Getty's men withdrew to the west, the Confederate commander gathered his chief officers around him to issue the orders that would place Cedar Creek at the very top of the list of great American military engagements and earn for Kershaw the nickname "Stonewall."

Maximum exploitation of the Cedar Creek success, Kershaw realized, depended on pressing after the Yankees to keep them on the run and deny them time to rally. To that end he ordered his lieutenants to push forward in pursuit as rapidly as possible. It took an hour or so for the Rebel officers to untangle their troops enough to set off in pursuit of the enemy, but by early afternoon the advance Confederate units were moving northward along the pike. As they went, the elated Rebels passed through the litter of dead horses and mules, smoldering wagons set afire by the retreating Federals, abandoned cannon, and discarded equipment and weapons thrown aside by the Northerners lest they slow the Yankee flight—the detritus of a beaten army. Many of Kershaw's soldiers paused briefly among the debris to snatch up food, clothing, or blankets before they hastened on to continue the chase.

Late that afternoon Wharton's Division, leading the Confederate column, routed a small Yankee rear guard in a brief action that went into the history books as the Third Battle of Kernstown. Nightfall found the advance units of Kershaw's army just south of Winchester. There the secessionists learned from some citizens who came out to the Rebel camps that the Northerners were preparing to make a stand on the hills and ridges south and southwest of the town.

Early the next morning Kershaw sent his divisions forward to assault the unionists' position. Getty's men, holding the center of the Yankee line, again put up a gallant fight, but most of the other Federal units had been completely demoralized by their crushing defeat on the previous day. When the armies collided, the Northerners could not long stand the strain. Slowly at first, and then with accelerating momentum, the blue ranks began to melt away. By midmorning the Fourth Battle of Winchester had ended. Getty, "the Rock of Cedar Creek," again found his division standing alone. With "Stonewall" Kershaw's victorious Rebels threatening to envelop both of his exposed flanks, he had no choice but to abandon the field and to retreat northward through the town. For the seventy-third time in the war Winchester changed hands.

Skillfully, Getty delayed the pursuing Confederates at every hill and stream for as long as possible. Behind the sturdy veterans of his Sixth Corps division, however, the remainder of Sheridan's panic-stricken army was in mad flight for the Potomac, its furious, cursing commander again swept along in the great tidal wave of retreat. By 10 o'clock that night, not a single organized Federal unit remained in the lower Shenandoah Valley. Sheridan, along with Wright and Ricketts, had disappeared in the fleeing mob as Getty desperately attempted to scrape together enough men to put up a respectable fight in the likely event that the Confederates crossed into Maryland and made another thrust at Washington.

News of the disaster in the Valley reached the Federal capital late on October 19, but it was almost noon of the following day before authorities began to get a real inkling of just how complete Sheridan's defeat had been. As additional reports trickled in, the government acted decisively. A curt telegram went out from the War Department to Sheridan relieving him, Wright, and Ricketts from command and reassigning all three of them to Minnesota, where they were to join Maj. Gen. John Pope in chasing the Sioux Indians.

Another dispatch informed Getty of his promotion to major general (with date of rank October 19) and directed him to assume command of what was left of the Army of the Shenandoah, gather up as many other men as he could find, and place his force in position east of the Monocacy River to meet the Rebels should they again cross the Potomac and descend on the Federal capital.

To Grant in front of Richmond went a third message instructing him to rush at least three additional infantry divisions northward by ship to aid in the defense of Washington. Once again, the Confederates had won a great success by playing their "Valley card."

PART TWO

Other Inconsequential
Engagements

E ven as Kershaw's Rebels swarmed through the streets of Winchester in pursuit of Sheridan's fleeing Yankees and as the town's civilians poured out of their houses and businesses to cheer their liberators, news of the secessionists' great victories flashed eastward by courier and telegraph to Lee and the Confederate authorities at Richmond. Lee, always alert to the opportunity to exploit any success to the utmost, soon learned from his spies and scouts that troops were leaving Grant's army in his front and correctly surmised that they were being summoned north to Washington to meet the threat posed by Kershaw's force in the lower Valley.

When Lee notified Kershaw that reinforcements from the Yankee lines at Richmond were on their way to the Federal capital, he also gave his subordinate free rein to cross into Maryland if circumstances indicated that such a raid could produce significant results. During the next day, as he maneuvered his troops northward toward the Potomac, "Stonewall" Kershaw pondered his options. Once he made his decision, secret orders went out to his subordinates and an encrypted message went east by telegraph to Lee.

Kershaw realized that heavily fortified Washington would be much too strong for his Rebels to capture, especially with its garrison strengthened by the three veteran divisions transferred from Grant's lines at Richmond and Petersburg. Even if somehow the Confederates could take the city, there was not very much they could do with it and they probably could not maintain possession of it for very long. The weakening of Grant's force before Richmond, however, seemed to offer the Southerners an excellent chance to repeat their great success of the spring and early summer of 1862, when they had concentrated their forces from the Valley and the Atlantic Coast to drive a Yankee army away from their capital.

Having come to this point in his thinking, Kershaw sent another secret telegram to Lee, this one proposing that he leave a small force in the lower Shenandoah Valley to demonstrate against the Yankees north of the Potomac while he and the balance of the Valley army moved to join Lee at Richmond. The combined Confederate forces would then assault the right flank of Grant's weakened line and attempt to drive the Federals away from the Rebel capital and Petersburg.

Lee had been thinking along the same lines, and he quickly concurred with Kershaw's proposal, directing "Stonewall" to move his troops to the Richmond area as quickly as possible. The Confederate commander optimistically set the twenty-seventh of October as the date for beginning the assault on the right end of Grant's long line. Such a tight schedule, he telegraphed Kershaw, would tax the men's endurance to the utmost. Lee knew, however, that it was imperative for the secessionists to strike before the troops Grant had sent to Washington could get back to the Yankee lines at Richmond. Every resource that the weakened Confederacy could muster would be employed to move Kershaw's men from the Valley and get them to the Richmond area on time.

Kershaw created what amounted to an ad hoc legion to leave in the lower Valley—a mixed command consisting of four regiments of cavalry, a battalion of horse artillery, and two regiments of infantry, plus Lt. Col. John S. Mosby's partisan rangers (43d Battalion of Virginia Cavalry). To command this force Kershaw selected Col. Thomas T. Munford of the 2d Virginia Cavalry Regiment. Munford received orders to keep the area as stirred up as possible in order to confuse the Federals and prevent them from learning what the Rebels were doing.

Over the next ten days, Munford carried out his mission with such zeal and success that for more than a week Washington authorities believed that Kershaw's entire force, which they estimated to number at least 45,000 men, was about to plunge into Maryland and, perhaps, push on into Pennsylvania. Alarmed, indeed almost hysterical Federal officials even badgered Grant to detach still more troops from the army at Richmond and send them to help protect Washington. Reports in the Richmond newspapers (planted by the Confederates to mislead the Yankees) that Lee had dispatched two of his veteran brigades to reinforce Kershaw in the Valley added to the uneasiness of official Washington.

By the time Union scouts managed to penetrate Munford's cavalry screen and bring back accurate and convincing intelligence about the Rebel force in the Valley, it was too late. For these brilliant services Munford received a promotion to brigadier general in December—a recognition that many thought long overdue.

While Munford toyed with the Yankees in Maryland and the lower Valley, "Stonewall" Kershaw's "foot cavalry" set new records for a troop movement. Utilizing wheezing locomotives and worn rail stock where possible and marching along on foot where the railroad had been torn up, the Rebel infantry hastened back up the Valley, turned east through the Blue Ridge, and headed for Richmond. At the Rebel capital, meanwhile, Lee and his lieutenants prepared for the great struggle that they knew would open once the Valley army arrived.

The Richmond-Petersburg front had been relatively quiet for several weeks, with no action that even approached the level of a large-scale skirmish. On October 26, however, a Union force thrust at the Rebel lines east of Richmond in a brief action that was called Second Oak Grove (also known as Second Henrico, Second King's School House, Second French's Field, and the Second Orchards). Only later would analysts of the war realize that it was the first of the series of engagements that collectively would become known as the Second Seven Days Battle.

On the following day Lee's great offensive against Grant's army got underway in earnest. During the midafternoon, Lt. Gen. Ambrose Powell Hill, whose Third Corps had been shifted from the extreme right end of the Confederate line below Petersburg to the left northeast of Richmond, lost patience when Kershaw was delayed by bad weather and did not arrive on schedule. At 3:00 P.M. a frustrated Hill sent his men across the Chickahominy River at Meadow Bridge and launched a premature attack on the Federals in what became known as the Second Battle of Mechanicsville (also called Second Ellison's [or Ellerson's] Mill and Second Beaver Dam Creek). Following a full and bloody but inconclusive afternoon of fighting, the Yankees pulled back a few miles to the old 1862 Gaines's Mill battlefield at Boatswain's Swamp (which had also been the site of the June 1864 engagement known as Cold Harbor).

On the twenty-eighth Kershaw finally reached his place on the left of Lee's battle line, and the entire Rebel force was united. Late that afternoon, following several unsuccessful piecemeal attacks, the Confederates launched a series of fierce, coordinated assaults on the unionists in the Second Battle of Gaines's Mill (also called Second Chickahominy and Third Cold Harbor). After a long day's conflict, a desperate Southern charge finally broke the Yankee line and sent the unionists reeling back across the Chickahominy.

Lee's great victory at Second Gaines's Mill tipped the balance against Grant. Realizing late on October 28 that he then faced a heavily reinforced Rebel army, the Yankee commander ordered a retreat down the James River, hoping to reach some point where he could find security from Lee's hammering attacks and support from the Federal gunboats in the river. This retreat—Grant always carefully referred to it as a "change of base"—got underway just as darkness fell that evening.

Over the next three days, Lee's pursuing secessionists nipped at the heels and right flank of Grant's withdrawing column as the unionists moved off down the James. The chief engagements came at Second Garnett's (also called Second Golding's Farm) on October 29; at Second Savage Station (also called Second Allen's Farm) on October 30; and at Second White Oak Swamp (also called Second Glendale, Second Charles City Road, and Second Frayser's Farm) on the thirty-first. By November 1, Grant's army was backed up on Malvern Hill, where on that day Lee made an unsuccessful assault on the Yankee lines.

Although his battered forces, with the assistance of several Union gunboats in the James River, had handily repulsed Lee's attacks at Second Malvern Hill, Grant soon realized that he could no longer continue his operations against Richmond and Petersburg. He therefore pulled his men back, continuing his movement down the James to the Westover area at Harrison's Landing (Berkeley Plantation).

On the morning of November 3, Maj. Gen. Wade Hampton, commanding the cavalry of Lee's army, rode up onto Evelington Heights, which overlooked and dominated the Harrison's Landing area. From that elevation, which the Yankees had neglected to occupy or even guard, Hampton saw immediately that Rebel artillery could sweep the Federal camps in the open area below. Sensing a great opportunity to damage the enemy, Hampton quietly deployed his horsemen to hold the height and sent staff officers and couriers hastening back to bring up every piece of artillery they could find. By patiently awaiting the arrival of the guns, Hampton was able to assemble some fifty cannon on the ridge by noon. At that hour he ordered the Rebel artillerymen to open fire.

Within minutes, exploding Confederate shells and ricocheting cannonballs produced great, if temporary, panic in Grant's camps. It took the Yankees some time to get their own artillery into action, move gunboats into position to shell the Southerners, and start a large force of infantry advancing up the ridge to drive the Rebels away. By then many areas of the camp were in flames. The bombardment caused only a few casualties, but the resulting fires consumed an estimated $800,000 worth of supplies and equipment. For Grant and the unionists, it was an embarrassing—even humiliating—coda to a campaign that had begun with such high hopes six months earlier.

While the Second Seven Days Battle raged outside Richmond, Federal authorities had ordered Maj. Gen. George Washington Getty, "the Rock of Cedar Creek," to move the remnant of Sheridan's old Army of the Shenandoah and whatever other commands he could scrape together into a fortified position on the left (northern) bank of the Rappahannock River near Fredericksburg.

Two weeks after the Evelington Heights fiasco, President Abraham Lincoln paid a visit to Grant's camps on the James. Following a long conference, the thoroughly demoralized chief executive ordered the disgraced Grant to transfer the beaten Army of the Potomac north by water from its base on the Peninsula to join the troops Getty was then organizing on the Rappahannock. Getty would assume command of the combined force (to be named the Army of Virginia) and begin preparations for the spring 1865 campaign, when the Yankees would launch yet one more "On to Richmond" drive. Once his troops had joined Getty, Grant, along with Meade and his chief subordinates from the Army of the Potomac, was to hasten to Minnesota to help Pope, Sheridan, Wright, and Ricketts chase the Sioux Indians.

Lee, meanwhile, had already shifted a division to the Fredericksburg area to observe Getty. When his scouts returned from down the James to report that Grant's units were embarking on troop transports, Lee concluded that they were bound for Getty's gathering army on the Rappahannock. The Confederate commander accordingly began to transfer the bulk of his own troops northward to position the Rebels so that they could meet any renewed effort that Getty might undertake.

By early December, Getty's newly organized Army of Virginia and Lee's Army of Northern Virginia were in camps along the Rappahannock where they had been when the bloody campaign of 1864 had begun seven months earlier—and where they had been encamped nineteen months earlier when the bloody campaigns of 1863 began. In fact, the two hostile armies were not far removed from where they had been thirty-one months earlier at the opening of the bloody campaigns of 1862. Indeed, they were not many miles distant from Manassas Junction where they had fought their first large battle in July 1861.

In December 1864 Lee, as he always did, wished to follow up his success by launching another campaign into Maryland and Pennsylvania— just as he had done after similar victories in 1862 and 1863. Sobering reports of his own losses in the Second Seven Days Battle, however, quickly convinced him that such an offensive then would be foolish in the extreme. Not only had the Army of Northern Virginia suffered some twenty thousand casualties in driving Grant and his forces away from Richmond and Petersburg but it had also lost vast quantities of equipment.

His transportation, Lee quickly realized, had been especially weakened in the late October engagements, and it simply was not possible for the Army of Northern Virginia to subsist for more than a day or so away from the railroad. In fact, Lee had serious doubts as to whether Virginia's badly damaged rail lines could even sustain his troops in the Fredericksburg area for very long.

Both of the leading modern authorities on this period of the war in Virginia agree with Lee on this point. Richard J. Sommers, in his *magnum opus, Richmond Redeemed Redux,* and Robert K. Krick, in his well-nigh definitive, award-winning seven-volume *Death Roster of Confederate Horses Killed in the Second Seven Days* as well as in his equally impressive and exhaustive three-volume *Lee's Mules: A Study in Transportation,* both come to the conclusion that Lee's army did not have the logistical capability to support even a small-scale operation beyond the Potomac in the early winter of 1864–65.

Lee and the Army of Northern Virginia had won yet another great victory in the Old Dominion. They had saved Richmond yet one more time and disposed of yet one more unsuccessful Yankee general. Once again, however, the Rebels found themselves too weak to follow up on their success.

The soldiers of both armies soon went to work building warm huts as they prepared once again to settle down into winter quarters beside the icy waters of the Rappahannock. While the men made ready for the winter, Lee and Getty kept themselves busy laboring to rebuild their forces for the coming spring's campaign.

PART THREE

Meanwhile

A week after the Second Seven Days Battle came to an end on the blood-drenched slopes of Malvern Hill, Northern voters went to the polls to elect a president. By that time news of the latest disaster to Federal arms in Virginia had spread across the country and newspapers were beginning to print the long, horrific casualty lists from the great battles outside Richmond. No effort by the Federal government could disguise the magnitude of Grant's losses in Virginia or the completeness of his failure there.

The late October casualties suffered by the Yankee army before Richmond, coupled with Sheridan's losses in the Valley and the men killed, wounded, and captured in Grant's spring, summer, and early fall battles, pushed total Union losses in Virginia for May–November 1864 to more than 155,000.

A bloodbath of that magnitude was simply too much for the Northern people, and they expressed their great discontent with the course of the war at the ballot box. George B. McClellan, the Democratic nominee for the presidency, running on a platform (adopted in late August) that branded the war a failure, carried every state except distant Oregon, which went for Lincoln by a vote of 9,888 to 8,457.

(Word of Grant's disaster before Richmond did not reach Oregon until after the polls there had closed on election day. When that state's citizens learned what had happened in Virginia, they petitioned for a new election. Disgusted members of the state legislature quickly passed a bill allowing the voters to cast ballots in a second presidential contest to be held on the first Tuesday after the first Monday in January 1865. The governor, however, vetoed the measure on the grounds that neither the state nor the Federal Constitution permitted voters to change their ballots after casting them and that even if the state did conduct such a second election, it would be a waste of time and money because a change of Oregon's electoral vote would have no effect on the results of the national balloting. This veto cost the otherwise very popular governor his own chance for reelection.)

The final official total popular vote count therefore stood at 2,218,493 for McClellan to 1,815,659 for Lincoln. The original projected vote in the Electoral College had been 230 for McClellan to 3 for Lincoln. Two of the frustrated Oregon electors, however, protested by casting their votes for retired general Winfield Scott, thereby making the final official tally 230 electoral votes for McClellan, 2 for Scott, and 1 for Lincoln. The resurgent Democrats also won solid majorities in both houses of Congress.

This overwhelming triumph over the hated Lincoln administration and congressional Republicans touched off a wild round of rejoicing among Northern Democrats, who saw their unbearable four-year exile in the political (patronage) wilderness finally coming to an end. As the magnitude of their election victory became clear, tens of thousands of Democrats poured out into the streets all across the North to celebrate by getting rip-roaring drunk.

Most of them did not sober up completely for two or three weeks, and accordingly not until near the end of November did the hangovers and the euphoria fade out enough for many of them once again to pay very much attention to news from the armies. When they did turn to recent military events, however, the Democrats, along with all other Northerners, found a series of rapidly developing news stories.

Some of the afternoon newspapers on December 1 published a telegram (soon reprinted in other journals) that had been received at the War Department at 3:40 that morning. The message, sent by Maj. Gen. George H. Thomas, commander of Union forces in Middle Tennessee, read:

> NASHVILLE, TENN. NOV. 30, 1864—11:30 P.M.
> Maj. Gen H. W. Halleck,
> Washington, D.C.:

I forward you the following dispatch containing good news from General [John M.] Schofield, at Franklin.

Franklin[, Tenn.], Nov. 30, 1864.

Major General Thomas:

The enemy made a heavy and persistent attack with about two corps, commencing at 4 p. m. and lasting until after dark. He was repulsed at all points, with very heavy loss, probably 5,000 or 6,000 men. Our loss is probably not more than one-tenth that number. We have captured about 1,000 men. . . .

J. M. SCHOFIELD,

Major-General.[1]

Two weeks of relative quiet followed, then happy Northerners delighted to read another message that had recently been received at the War Department. It too came from the West:

NASHVILLE, TENN., December 15, 1864—9 P.M.

Maj. Gen. Halleck,

Washington, D.C.

I attacked the enemy's left this morning and drove it . . . about eight miles. Have captured . . . a . . . train of about 20 wagons with between 800 and 1,000 prisoners and 16 pieces of artillery. I shall attack the enemy again to-morrow. . . .

GEO. H. THOMAS,

Major-General U.S. Volunteers, Commanding.[2]

On December 17 even more cheering news reached the national capital:

HEADQUARTERS, DEPARTMENT OF THE CUMBERLAND,

Eight Miles from Nashville, December 16, 1864—6 P.M.

---

1. U.S. War Department, *The War of the Rebellion: A Compilation of the Official Records of the Union and Confederate Armies,* 128 vols. (Washington, D.C.: GPO, 1880–1901), ser. 1, vol. 45, 1:1167 (hereafter cited as *OR,* with all references to volumes in series 1).

2. *OR,* vol. 45, 2:194.

... the enemy has been pressed at all points to-day. . . . Brigadier-General [Edward] Hatch, . . . on the right, turned the enemy's left, and captured a large number of prisoners. . . . Schofield's troops . . . carried several heights, captured many prisoners and six pieces of artillery. . . . [Andrew J.] Smith carried the salient point of the enemy's line . . . capturing 16 pieces of artillery, 2 brigadier generals, and about 2,000 prisoners. . . . [Kenner] Garrard's division . . . carried the enemy's intrenchments, capturing all the artillery and troops of the enemy on the line. . . . [Thomas J.] Wood's corps . . . took up the assault, carrying the enemy's intrenchments in his front, captured 8 pieces of artillery, something over 600 prisoners. . . . I am glad to be able to state that the number of prisoners captured yesterday greatly exceeds the number reported by me last evening. The woods, fields, and intrenchments are strewn with the enemy's small arms, abandoned in their retreat. . . .

GEO. H. THOMAS,

Major-General, U.S. Volunteers, Commanding[3]

Over the following week additional dispatches from Thomas streamed into Washington as his victorious forces pursued the fleeing Confederates southward toward the Tennessee River, gobbling up hundreds of prisoners along with abandoned guns, wagons, and other equipment. On December 18 Thomas was at Spring Hill, some thirty-two miles south of Nashville, but there heavy rains slowed the pursuit. On the twentieth he drove the secessionist rear guard over the Duck River at Columbia. Two days later Thomas's pontoon train caught up with his army, and he was able to cross the Duck and resume the chase.

For the next few days the Federals kept after the defeated and demoralized Southerners, but again rain, mud, extended supply lines, and exhausted men, mules, and horses along with a heroic Rebel rear guard slowed the effort. Eventually, the Confederates managed to put the broad Tennessee River between themselves and their pursuers, but their de-

3. Ibid., 210–11.

feat in Tennessee had been total. Confederate power west of the Appalachian Mountains had been broken for all time.[4]

As the now-gleeful Northerners closely followed the reports of Thomas's great successes in Middle Tennessee, they also received encouraging news from another front. On December 25 Washington authorities released to the press a message recently received from Maj. Gen. William T. Sherman, whose 65,000 troops had marched out of the captured city of Atlanta in mid-November and continued, virtually unopposed, across Georgia to the sea. Dated Savannah, Georgia, December 22 and addressed to President Lincoln, the message read: "I beg leave to present you as a Christmas present the City of Savannah with 150 heavy guns and plenty of ammunition and also about 25,000 bales of cotton."[5]

Pausing only briefly at Savannah to resupply his troops from the Union ships that had been hovering off the coast but now could come upriver into the port, Sherman took advantage of the fine weather during early January 1865 to resume his march. He crossed the Savannah River into South Carolina and occupied Columbia, the state capital, on the seventeenth of the month. A great fire the following day (origins unknown but much debated) destroyed a large part of the city. Meanwhile, Sherman's progress through South Carolina compelled the Confederates to evacuate Charleston on January 18 lest the city's garrison find itself cut off and forced to surrender. The Union navy and the Federal troops who had been serving on the coastal islands quickly occupied the city where secession had begun in December 1860.

In early February, Sherman's mighty column swept across the state line and entered North Carolina. On the eleventh the Yankees occupied Fayetteville and destroyed the Confederate government arms works and other public buildings there. Four days later they crossed the Cape Fear River and closed on Goldsboro. Their advance forced the Rebels to abandon Wilmington, the Confederacy's last open port on the Atlantic. On February 19, 20, and 21, a rag-tag collection of secessionist units, pulled together from all over the West, joined by the Atlantic coastal garrisons,

4. Ibid., 228–29, 249–50, 265, 283–84, 307–8, 319, 369–70.
5. *OR,* vol. 44, 1:783.

and commanded by Gen. Joseph E. Johnston, staged a delaying action against Sherman's horde near Bentonville. After a brief engagement, the Union juggernaut brushed its opponents aside and rolled on.

Reinforced by forty thousand troops transferred to the North Carolina coast from Thomas's army in Tennessee, Sherman continued his march. Dispatching a small column westward to occupy Raleigh, the state capital, he pushed northward toward Virginia with his main force. Johnston and his small Confederate army retreated in the face of Sherman's advancing Yankees. "There was," Sherman was to write a decade later, "no force in existence that could delay our progress."[6]

Shortly before 11:00 A.M. on March 2, the morning train from Richmond, as usual running some two hours late, puffed up to the low platform a few miles south of Fredericksburg that then served the area as a temporary station. (The town's railroad depot had long since been destroyed along with much of the track in the nearby area.) Among the arriving passengers was a stocky, grayish officer, just below medium height, some fifty-five or sixty years of age. Slowly he climbed down from the cars, soon procured a horse, mounted, and rode off to find the headquarters of the Army of Northern Virginia. The visitor was Gen. Joseph E. Johnston's favorite staff officer, his faithful adjutant, Col. Simon Craig.

A Military Academy classmate of Lee and Johnston (Class of 1829), Craig had resigned from the army four years after his graduation to manage his family's extensive property in Florida. He had married well, prospered as a planter, and held several local political offices. After opposing secession in early 1861, Craig had returned to military duty, securing an appointment first in the Florida state forces and then in the Confederate army. A few weeks after entering Confederate service, he had received an assignment to Johnston's staff, and all of his subsequent duty had been in that capacity. Now, his general had sent him to Lee with a confidential message.

6. William T. Sherman, *Memoirs of General William T. Sherman by Himself*, 2 vols. (1875; reprint, Bloomington: Indiana Univ. Press, 1957), 2:307.

Craig reached Lee's headquarters about 12:30 P.M. and dismounted. He found his old classmate in conference with his corps commanders, but when Lee learned of his visitor's presence, he summoned Craig into his tent and introduced him to Kershaw, Gordon, Hill, and his other chief subordinates and members of his staff. After chatting briefly, the others departed.

Once the two old friends were alone, Craig delivered Johnston's communication. It was, Lee quickly realized, a very pessimistic letter. Sherman, Johnston wrote, with a force estimated at 95,000 men was then approaching the border between North Carolina and Virginia and would soon assail Petersburg and Richmond from the south. Thomas, with a column from Middle Tennessee believed by the Confederates to number at least 60,000, was moving through East Tennessee and into southwest Virginia. This force obviously would operate against the Richmond-Petersburg area from the west. On the north side of the Rappahannock stood Maj. Gen. George W. Getty, "the Rock of Cedar Creek," and his Army of Virginia—a force of at least 80,000.

His own troops, Johnston declared in his letter, could do no more. If his army moved east, it would find itself penned against the Atlantic Ocean and the Union navy. If it continued retreating northward, it would back through Petersburg, Richmond, and Lee's army into Getty. If it turned westward, it would encounter Thomas's powerful force. Should it march to the south, it would meet Sherman's advancing columns.

At this point Lee looked up from the paper he was reading. A slight smile flickered briefly across his face. "Well, Si," he chuckled, "that last would certainly take Sherman by surprise." Adjusting his spectacles, Lee then turned once again to Johnston's letter.

In summary, Johnston wrote, the Confederacy had been reduced to a shrinking rectangle in eastern and south-central Virginia. Rebel forces in the area—his and Lee's armies—numbered at most only about 60,000 men. Soldiers from the Deep South, he reported, were deserting from his ranks almost en masse every day. Soon he and Lee would find themselves completely cut off from all outside sources of food, ammunition, clothing, shoes, and medicines. The Confederate government had no more reinforcements to throw into the fight. Within a week or two, enemy forces numbering at least 200,000 men would surround the two great Rebel armies. The secessionists would find themselves trapped as well as outnumbered by more than three to one (and most of these unionists, Johnston pointed out, "would not be your effeminate Eastern Yankees").

Faced with this clearly hopeless situation, Johnston went on, he was unwilling to bear the responsibility for any more deaths, suffering, and destruction. If President Jefferson Davis and Lee determined to continue the struggle, he would obey orders and do his best, but he did not wish to have on his hands the blood of his soldiers killed and wounded in a useless effort. The better course, Johnston concluded, would be for the Confederates to abandon their quest for independence and to surrender. He, therefore, closed by urging Lee to see Davis, convince the president of the hopelessness of their cause and the futility (even crime) of further resistance, and request authorization to cease hostilities. The alternative, he added, would be useless battles that would bring needless deaths and injuries to the soldiers and even more suffering and destruction to Virginia and her people. The hundreds or thousands of men lost or crippled in such meaningless warfare, he predicted, would be the best, brightest, and bravest left in the South.

When he finished reading Johnston's letter, Lee put it down, removed his glasses, rubbed his eyes, and bowed his head. After several minutes of painful silence, he asked Craig to leave him alone for two hours. Once his old classmate had gone to find some food and take a short nap, the general sat in silence, lost in his own thoughts.

Lee's mind ran back over the events of the last four years. The agonizing decision to resign from the "old army" and go with his native Virginia had been followed by the hectic first weeks in the Confederacy and then by the frustrating months in western Virginia and along the South Atlantic Coast. In the spring of 1862 he had been recalled to an even more frustrating desk job in Richmond. His real chance had come the following June when the president had named him to command the main Confederate army in Virginia after Johnston had been severely wounded in the Battle of Seven Pines.

Once in command of what he came to call the Army of Northern Virginia, Lee had achieved a spectacular string of victories, driving the Federals away from Richmond and managing within a year to shift temporarily the war in the East from the banks of the James to the banks of the Susquehanna. In 1864 he had waged the great campaign against Grant, which had culminated in the bloody triumph of the Second Seven Days.

Quickly the scenes followed one another through his mind: the great assault of June 27, 1862 at First Gaines's Mill (First Cold Harbor) that had given him victory over George McClellan in his initial major campaign; the giddy triumph at Second Manassas when John Pope's beaten Yankee army had fled from the field; the desperate hours along the Antietam as he furiously shifted troops from point to point on his line to repel one attack after another by McClellan's army; the magnificent, doomed Yankee assaults that Ambrose Burnside had launched against his position at Fredericksburg; the spectacular victory over Joseph Hooker at Chancellorsville; Pettigrew's and Pickett's men following their blood-red battleflags up the fiery slope at Gettysburg; the terrible fighting in the Wilderness when the gunfire set the woods aflame and hundreds of the wounded had burned to death; the horrific Battle of the Crater; and then the last, long, bloody campaign against Grant outside Richmond.

So many had been killed or wounded: the immortal "Stonewall" Jackson—now in his grave almost two years—had fallen at Chancellorsville, cut down by the bullets of his own men; "Jeb" Stuart, the laughing cavalier, had taken his mortal wound a year later at Yellow Tavern; Charles Winder had been killed at Cedar Mountain; Dorsey Pender and Lewis Armistead had received mortal wounds at Gettysburg, and Dick Garnett and so many others had died there; Robert Rodes had fallen at Third Winchester; Early and Ramseur at Cedar Creek; "the gallant" youth John Pelham at Kelly's Ford. The list went on and on and on. And then there were the wounded—Richard Ewell, James Longstreet, Wade Hampton, James Kemper, John B. Gordon, John Bell Hood.

Hood's name shifted Lee's reverie into a new channel. Lee had first met the young Kentuckian in the early 1850s when he had been the superintendent of the Military Academy and Hood a cadet. Later the two had served together in Texas as officers in the grand old 2d U.S. Cavalry Regiment, and Lee had become something of a father figure for the young lieutenant. In 1862, as a brigade and then a division commander, Hood had proved himself to be one of the best young officers in Lee's army. He took a serious wound at Gettysburg in July 1863 and an even more serious injury at Chickamauga two months later. Then, with a useless, withered left arm and an artificial right leg, he had gone back into battle, and in July 1864 President Davis had selected him to command the Army of Tennessee, the main Confederate force in the West.

The West! Damn the West! On April 10, 1862, Lee had written, "If [the] Mississippi Valley is lost [the] Atlantic States will be ruined." Even as his army had more than held its own in Virginia over the next two and one-half years, he had watched in dismay as battle by battle the Confederacy's western armies had yielded not only the Mississippi Valley but also Kentucky, Missouri, and almost all of Tennessee, Arkansas, Louisiana, and Mississippi. In early 1864 Lee had commented, "I believe . . . that . . . if Mississippi and Tennessee [could be] recovered, it would do more to relieve the country and inspirate our people than the mere capture of Washington." Over the next twelve months the western Rebels had not only failed to recover Mississippi and Tennessee but they had also lost Alabama, Georgia, and the Carolinas. Damn the West![7]

Lee dropped to his knees and began to pray.

At about 4:00 P.M. Lee asked his orderly to summon Craig. When his old friend appeared, rubbing sleep from his eyes, Lee invited him into the tent. Taking a deep breath, the general admitted that there could be no

---

7. *OR,* vol. 6:423; vol. 32, 2:566. Compare Lee's 1862 prediction with Lincoln's June 30, 1862, observation, "To take and hold the railroad east of Cleveland in East Tennessee, I think fully as important as the taking and holding of Richmond"; Halleck's comment on March 20, 1863, "In my opinion, the opening of the Mississippi River will be to us of more advantage than the capture of forty Richmonds," and with Sherman's boast of March 10, 1864, "from the West, when our task is done, we will make short work of Charleston and Richmond and the impoverished coast of the Atlantic." *OR,* vol. 16, 2:75; vol. 24, 1:22; vol. 32, 3:49.

denying the truth of Johnston's assertions. Tears welled up in his eyes. "General Johnston is correct," Lee stammered. "We face overwhelming numbers and resources. It would be a criminal act to subject the brave survivors of so many hard fought battles who have remained steadfast to the last to the loss that must attend the continuance of the contest. We must avoid the useless sacrifice of those whose past services have endeared them to their countrymen. I shall go to Richmond and see the President."

Before boarding the southbound train, Lee directed Craig to telegraph Johnston requesting that he meet Lee in the capital. As an afterthought, Craig added his own suggestion that if Generals Pierre G. T. Beauregard and Braxton Bragg and Johnston's chief subordinates, Lieutenant Generals William J. Hardee, Alexander P. Stewart, and Wade Hampton, agreed as to the hopelessness of the Confederate cause, they too should come to Richmond.

Lee reached the capital shortly after midnight. Early the next morning (March 3) he, Johnston, Beauregard, Bragg, Hardee, Stewart, and Hampton called on Secretary of War John C. Breckinridge at the War Department. After listening to the generals, the secretary confessed that for some time he too had believed the cause lost. At their request, Breckinridge accompanied the seven generals when they went to the Executive Mansion on Clay Street for their 11:00 A.M. appointment with the president.

Davis, wholeheartedly committed to the cause of Southern independence, at first stoutly resisted the recommendation of his secretary of war and his generals. As the day wore along, however, he gradually came to admit the truth of their assertions about both the hopelessness of the Confederacy's position and the need to preserve as many lives as possible to rebuild the South after the war. Shortly after 7:00 that evening, he reluctantly acquiesced and authorized Lee to arrange for the surrender of all Confederate forces still in the field.

The fourth of March 1865 dawned cloudy in Washington, D.C., but just before noon, as President-elect McClellan emerged from the Capitol to take the oath of office as the nation's seventeenth chief executive, a bright sun broke through the clouds and bathed the inaugural platform in a warm winter light.

A few seconds before McClellan was to begin the oath, a breathless clerk from the War Department pushed his way onto the platform and handed a telegram to President Lincoln. As Lincoln read the document, a wan smile crossed his face—the first in many months. The president passed the dispatch to McClellan. The message was from Getty on the Rappahannock. It announced that he had just received, under flag of truce, from Lee a note stating that the Confederates would agree to surrender that afternoon.

One modern writer, with but slight exaggeration, has called George B. McClellan "the only man who would fold with a royal flush."[8] Even McClellan, however, could grasp the meaning of this dispatch. Returning the message to Lincoln, he stepped in front of Chief Justice Salmon P. Chase, placed his left hand on a Bible, and raised his right.

Thus, by midafternoon on March 4, 1865, the nation stood reunited after almost exactly four years of civil war. To be sure, the country faced enormous problems adjusting its racial, constitutional, political, economic, cultural, and social institutions to the new conditions created by the conflict. The basic military problem, however, had been solved. The Union had been preserved.

8. Bob Thornsberry, "Lousy Civil War Leaders," *The Minie News* 265 (Apr. 1996): 6.

PART FOUR

The Big Picture

My purpose in writing the foregoing counterfactual essay has not been to produce a detailed tactical study of an imaginary Civil War battle or military campaign or even to suggest that the fictitious events narrated in Parts 1, 2, and 3 could have taken place. Frankly, I find hyperdetailed tactical military micronarratives mind numbing, and I will be the first to admit that the military campaigns described in the preceding parts could not have happened.

Logistical considerations alone (not to mention the physical limits of human endurance) would have made it impossible for any troops to perform most of the feats of marching and fighting that I attribute to Kershaw's "foot cavalry." Lee, of course, would have been most reluctant to interject his own ideas into such a political topic as the discussion of a possible national surrender. On one occasion late in the war, he declined even to express an opinion as to where the Rebels should relocate their national capital in the event they were compelled to evacuate Richmond because that question was a "political matter." In February 1865 he told Maj. Gen. John B. Gordon that he "scarcely felt authorized to suggest to the civil authorities the advisability of making terms with the Government of the United States."[1]

Jefferson Davis, of course, would have been very unwilling to accept defeat even under the circumstances portrayed in this essay. Nor did

1. Gordon, *Reminiscences,* 390. Civil War generals' memoirs should be used with extreme care—especially Gordon's. There is, in fact, some evidence that Lee, Secretary of War Breckinridge, and perhaps others may have attempted to nudge President Davis toward surrender in March 1865. William C. Davis, *Breckinridge: Statesman, Soldier, Symbol* (Baton Rouge: Louisiana State Univ. Press, 1974), 496–98; William C. Davis, conversations with author. If Gordon did not make up the incident, it may have been that Lee changed his mind after the conversation, made the statement at an earlier date, or—most likely— simply chose not to discuss such a delicate matter with his subordinate, even one as prominent as Gordon had become by early 1865.

Sherman begin his advance northward from Savannah until early February 1865 because the January weather, in fact, was very bad that year. Thus, all of his 1865 exploits described in Part 3 have been advanced by one month.

Although many of the particulars narrated in Parts 1, 2, and 3 are beyond the range of possibility, something quite similar to the *results* I ascribe to them could have been produced by less far-fetched events that fall well within the limits of the possible.

Suppose, for example, that Grant had been decapitated by a stray cannonball on the morning of May 6, 1864, as he sat in his headquarters camp beside the Germanna Road eating his breakfast (a cup of strong coffee and a sliced cucumber doused with vinegar, after which he enjoyably smoked a cigar).[2] Might his less resolute successor, Maj. Gen. Ambrose E. Burnside, have ordered a retreat later that day when the Confederates launched fierce attacks first against his left flank and then against his right?[3]

Or suppose that Lee had enjoyed excellent health on May 23, 24, and 25 when Grant sent his troops across the North Anna River. At that time the Confederate army held a short, heavily entrenched position along the right (south) bank of the river at Ox Ford, with both wings of its strong fortifications bent back from the stream at angles of about forty-five degrees and extending southeast and southwest almost to the Little River. The Rebel position resembled an inverted "V," with the point on the North Anna at the ford.

Upon reaching the stream, Grant crossed his forces to either side of the secessionists' river line and in so doing impaled his army on Lee's trenches. Two difficult river crossings separated the wings of the Yankee army, and Lee's veterans occupied impregnable fortifications between the isolated parts of Grant's force. Had the Rebels struck at one part of

2. Horace Porter, *Campaigning with Grant* (New York: Century, 1897), 56.

3. Burnside was the ranking major general with the forces then under Grant's direct control. His unit, the Ninth Corps, however, was technically not a part of the Army of the Potomac, which was commanded by Maj. Gen. George G. Meade. Even had the cautious and more capable Meade, rather than Burnside, taken Grant's place, he might well have fallen back in the face of Lee's May 6 assaults on his flanks.

the Union army while it was separated from the other, they might well have inflicted a stunning defeat on that portion before the other Federals could have come to its aid.

As it turned out, of course, all of the cannonballs missed Grant's head on May 6 and Lee was so prostrated by illness (diarrhea) on May 23, 24, and 25 that he could not take advantage of Grant's blunder at the North Anna. Nor did he then have any subordinate whom he could have entrusted with command of the army. The Confederate commander lay incapacitated in his tent during those days, moaning, "We must strike them a blow—we must never let them pass us again." Meanwhile, Grant realized his predicament, pulled his army back to safety, and soon marched off to the east and south to try once again (without success, as it turned out) to swing around Lee's right flank.

Even so, had Grant been killed during the campaign that summer or had the Southerners won a tactical victory that compelled the unionists to retreat into the Washington fortifications, the *ultimate military outcome of the war* would not have changed. Even had Lincoln lost the 1864 election to McClellan, the Federal armies would have been so close to final victory by March 1865, when the new president would have assumed office, that there could have been no rational doubt about the ultimate triumph of the national government. (This argument, of course, assumes that Lincoln would not have done something foolish between the election in November 1864 and McClellan's inauguration four months later and thereby lost a war that his armies had already won. McClellan, we should not forget, had pledged in September 1864—*after* the capture of Atlanta—that as president he would continue the war if such a policy was necessary to preserve the Union.)

How could this be? Would not a great Rebel victory over Grant in Virginia in 1864, especially if coupled with the defeat of Lincoln at the ballot box that November, have led to Confederate independence? The answer is clearly "no," and an understanding of this seeming paradox requires of many students of the war a "paradigm shift." They simply must learn to look at the big picture of the war and to think about the war's overall military history in a different way.

In Washington sometime during Tuesday, December 30, 1862, Edward Bates, attorney general in President Abraham Lincoln's cabinet, sat down at his desk to compose the day's entry in his diary. Thinking back over the events of the year then just closing, the pessimistic Bates took up his pen and wrote: "we have not suppressed the rebellion. We have, during the whole of the year, made no important advance toward its suppression. On the contrary, our present position is relatively worse than it was last spring."[4]

As the discouraged Bates penned these lines, he doubtless had in mind the recent (December 13) crushing defeat that Lee had administered to the Federal army at Fredericksburg, only about fifty miles south of Washington, and its attendant 12,500 Yankee casualties. He may, although it seems unlikely, have known also of the even more recent (December 29) repulse of Union forces at Walnut Hills (Chickasaw Bluffs) on the Yazoo River and of the failure of the first Northern efforts against Vicksburg, Mississippi. Whether Bates knew of the recent defeat in Mississippi or not, his diary entry reflects the common "Virginia-centric" view of the war that led to so much misunderstanding of the military operations of the North-South conflict in the 1860s and that still hampers so many of those who seek to understand how the war unfolded.

Bates wrote those sentences near the end of a year that, in fact, *had* seen the national armies, with the considerable help of the Union navy, make great strides toward suppressing the rebellion. At the beginning of 1862 the secessionists had control of the Mississippi River from Columbus, Kentucky, south to the Gulf of Mexico. They then maintained sizable military forces in Kentucky and Missouri and, in fact, had sponsored pro-secession governments in those two states and admitted both of them into the Confederacy. Except for isolated, mountainous western Virginia and a few small enclaves in the northern and eastern parts of the Old Dominion and a few more along the Atlantic and Gulf coasts, Confederate territory was free of invading Union troops on January 1, 1862.

---

4. Bates, *The Diary of Edward Bates, 1859–1866,* ed. Howard K. Beale (Washington, D.C.: GPO, 1933; reprint, New York: DaCapo, 1975), 272.

The Rebels' situation had changed dramatically by the time Bates made his diary entry for December 30. During the year, Northern armies had chased the secessionists out of both Kentucky and Missouri and permanently restored the national authority in those states, although both remained open to occasional Rebel incursions for the remainder of the war. Only the short stretch of the Mississippi River between Vicksburg and Port Hudson, Louisiana, remained in Confederate hands at the end of 1862. Yankee armies then occupied West and much of Middle Tennessee as well as important parts of Arkansas, Louisiana, Mississippi, and Alabama.

As 1862 came to its end, gunboats of the U.S. Navy ranged at will along the navigable section of the Cumberland River as far up as Nashville and as far up the Tennessee River as the Florence-Tuscumbia area in northwestern Alabama, where the "Shoals" in the river—not the secessionists—brought their progress to a halt. The crucial town of Corinth, Mississippi, had fallen to the Federals, and when it did the Yankees cut the Memphis & Charleston Railroad, the South's one true east-west rail line. Nashville, Memphis, New Orleans, and Pensacola had all passed permanently into Northern hands.

The Union troops who failed in their first efforts to take Vicksburg in December 1862 had spent the previous December in northern Kentucky, southern Illinois, and east-central Missouri. They would celebrate New Years Day, 1863, deep in Confederate territory—very close, in fact, to the geographic center of Rebeldom. Even as Bates scribbled in his diary that next-to-last day of the old year, a great battle was taking shape near Murfreesboro, Tennessee, some thirty miles southeast of Nashville. When it ended late on January 2, 1863, the Confederates would retreat again and one more important slice of secessionist territory would pass permanently back under Federal control.

In truth, 1862 had been a year of great military success for Union arms. Attorney General Bates, like so many people then and later, simply wore blinders that prevented his seeing the war outside Virginia.[5]

---

5. Several years ago, during a talk at a Civil War symposium in Hagerstown, Maryland, I made passing reference to the Rebels' great defeats in 1862. Afterward, a gentleman accosted

Those who seek to *understand* the military history of the Civil War, then, must abandon the apparently eternal quest for ever more detailed minutiae about the numerous battles waged in Virginia (along with the great engagements in Maryland and Pennsylvania—Antietam and Gettysburg).

To be sure, those eastern battles brim with human-interest stories and, for those drawn to such a topic, sometimes fascinating tactical details (as, in fact, do the western, coastal, naval, and Trans-Mississippi battles). The cumulative result of the eastern engagements, however, was a bloody strategic stalemate that began in the summer of 1861 and continued right up to the last week or so of the Confederacy's existence. Neither side could win the war in the Old Dominion so long as Robert E. Lee lived, and neither side could lose it there—as the war was fought. Had the fighting been limited to Virginia (I sometimes say half-facetiously), it would still be going on, with the Army of the Potomac and the Army of Northern Virginia preparing to fight the Thirty-sixth Battle of Manassas or the Eighty-third Battle of Winchester.

> Imaginary conversation between two Northerners in May 2017:
> A: "Yikes! I hope we can defeat Lee this summer."
> B: "Me too. That old man has been beating up on us now for 155 years. I thought Ike had him back in '45 with that atomic bomb. I *still* don't see how he got out of that one!"

Fortunately for all of us (and, considering the role the United States played in the twentieth century, for the rest of the world as well), the

---

me with the question, "What battles did the South lose in 1862?" He, of course, like Bates, was thinking in terms of Virginia—"Stonewall" Jackson's brilliant campaign in the Shenandoah Valley, the Seven Days Battle, Cedar Mountain, Second Manassas, Antietam (a tactical victory for the Confederates), and Fredericksburg. I think he was somewhat stunned at my quick answer to his question: "Mill Springs, Fort Henry, Fort Donelson, Pea Ridge, Shiloh, Island Number Ten, Forts Jackson and St. Philip, Plum Run Bend, Memphis, Baton Rouge, Iuka, Corinth, Perryville (a strategic defeat for the Rebels but a limited tactical victory), Prairie Grove, and Stones River." Clearly, he knew very little about any of those engagements and probably had never heard of some of them. Yet all of them—unlike the battles in Virginia that year—had important and *lasting* military results. One well-known modern historian has recently commented that "People who follow the war in the West at least know that there were battles in the East."

war was not confined to the Old Dominion. As the Army of Northern Virginia and the Army of the Potomac struggled back and forth across east-central Virginia, the military events that were to bring about the defeat of the Confederacy, the preservation of the Union, and the emancipation of American slaves, as well as lay the foundation for America's emergence as a world power, were rapidly unfolding elsewhere.

In the summer of 1861 Wilmer McLean lived on a fourteen-hundred-acre plantation situated along a northern Virginia creek called Bull Run. The first large-scale engagement of the war took place along that stream on July 21, 1861. Three days before the battle, an artillery shell crashed through McLean's house during some of the preliminary skirmishing. After the battle, dead and wounded men littered the yard and fields around the McLean home, and the house itself served as a hospital.

The experience proved too much for McLean. To escape further involvement in the war, he decided to move his family away from the area of hostilities. Eventually, he settled some one hundred miles to the southwest in the little village of Appomattox Court House. To his newer residence came Lee and Grant on the morning of April 9, 1865, to sign the documents that provided for the surrender of the Army of Northern Virginia, which, for most people, symbolizes the end of the war.

In his later years McLean is supposed to have quipped that the Civil War began in his front yard and ended in his parlor.

Almost all of the crucial military events that brought Lee and Grant to the McLean house on April 9, 1865, took place months before that spring day, and most of them occurred hundreds of miles beyond the borders of the Old Dominion. Union and Confederate forces waged the battles that determined the military outcome of the war along the Mississippi, the Cumberland, and the Tennessee Rivers, not on the banks of the Rappahannock, the Shenandoah, and the James; at Dover, Vicksburg, Chattanooga, and Atlanta, not at Manassas, Richmond, Sharpsburg, and Gettysburg. While the two great armies in Virginia fought their way from Wilmer McLean's front yard to his parlor, other great armies fought their way from the Ohio River to the Gulf of Mexico, from the Mississippi

Valley to the Atlantic Coast, and from the mouth of the Ogeechee River on the Georgia coast below Savannah to Raleigh, North Carolina.

Understanding these facts and their importance is the "paradigm shift" that many students of the war will have to make if they are to comprehend why and how the South lost and why and how the North won the Civil War. Once they change the point from which they view the sectional struggle, they will discover that the conflict as seen from St. Louis, Louisville, Chattanooga, or Montgomery takes on quite a different appearance from the way it looks if it is viewed only from the narrow, provincial confines of Washington and Richmond. As Robin Williams's character observed in the movie *Dead Poets Society*, "We must constantly look at things in a different way."

⇥ PART FIVE ⇤

Implications

Acceptance of what we may call the "western paradigm" as the new framework for interpreting the military history of the Civil War enables us to put the conflict's battles and campaigns into perspective and in so doing arrive at what I believe to be a better comprehension of the overall history of the struggle. The new paradigm can also give us a different (and I think more valid) view of several controversial issues of greater or lesser importance. In that way it will help us historians answer some crucial questions and achieve a better understanding not only of the North-South conflict itself but also of the relative importance of several wartime events and of the roles that some prominent individuals played in the sectional struggle.

Why (or How) Did the Confederacy Lose (or the Federal Government Win) the War?

Over the decades since the end of the war, this question in one form or another has generated a great deal of controversy. In another fifteen hundred years or so, we should have a body of historical literature devoted to this subject that will equal (and may very well exceed) in quantity that dealing with the history of the decline and fall of the Roman Empire.

Almost as soon as the war came to an end in the spring of 1865, many of the defeated Confederates began seeking the reason (or reasons) for their failure. Thousands of the disappointed Rebels immediately grasped at the "overwhelming numbers and resources" explanation initially put forth in Gen. Robert E. Lee's "Farewell Order" to his army (General Orders No. 9, Headquarters, Army of Northern Virginia, April 10, 1865): "After four years of arduous service, marked by unsurpassed courage and fortitude, the Army of Northern Virginia has been compelled to yield to overwhelming numbers and resources."

Since that long-ago spring, whole battalions of historians have kept themselves occupied adding details to Lee's assertion. They have compiled a long list of categories in all of which the North enjoyed a clear and often overwhelming superiority over the South. Examples include population, hoes, boots and shoes, ships (both merchant and naval), railroad mileage and rolling stock, the value of real and personal property, textiles, agricultural machinery, firearms, factories of various kinds, industrial workers (1,300,000 as opposed to 110,000 in the South in 1860), iron foundries, financial capital, immigrants, and many others. "Why, all we have," Rhett Butler told a group of his fellow Southerners in the spring of 1861 during the barbecue at Twelve Oaks, "is cotton and slaves and arrogance."[1]

In recent years, however, the "overwhelming numbers" explanation itself has fallen out of favor among modern historians, who can cite several instances of wars in which the weaker side prevailed over the stronger—the experience of the United States in Vietnam being among the more recent.

A few years after Robert E. Lee's death in October 1870, a group of former Confederates (almost all of them Virginians) led by ex–lieutenant general Jubal A. Early developed a second explanation for the Rebels' military failure. In the crucial Battle of Gettysburg, they asserted, Lt. Gen. James Longstreet, the senior corps commander in Lee's army, had made numerous mistakes, dawdled when he should have been hurrying his troops into the battle, and even withheld wholehearted cooperation from Lee—if, indeed, he did not directly disobey Lee's orders. Longstreet's failures and insubordination, Early and his disciples implied, had cost the Southerners victory at Gettysburg in July 1863 and had led ultimately to the surrender at Appomattox Court House in April 1865.

For many of the old Rebels, the "Longstreet lost it all at Gettysburg" theme quickly took its place alongside Lee's "overwhelming numbers

1. Margaret Mitchell, *Gone with the Wind* (New York: Macmillan, 1936), 101.

and resources" explanation for the South's failure to win its independence. To those who accepted—and to some degree expanded on—Early's arguments, the historical reasons for Confederate defeat came to rest on those two assertions. In a brilliant analogy, historian Gaines M. Foster has compared the activities of "Early and company" to the late-nineteenth-century ghost dance of the Plains Indians. "Formed in a circle . . . , the true believers dance in and back, chanting, on one foot, 'overwhelmed by numbers' and on the other 'betrayed by Longstreet.'"[2]

After the war, Longstreet, unlike most former Confederates, became a Republican and urged his fellow white Southerners to accept the results of their battlefield defeat. Such counsel rankled many of the former Rebels, who were still dazed by and bitter at the outcome of the conflict and angered and frightened by the postwar racial policies of the national Republican party.

To make matters worse, at least so far as "Early and company" were concerned, Longstreet was not a Virginian, but during the war the rules of military seniority had worked so that he ranked second only to Lee in the command hierarchy of the Army of Northern Virginia. Longstreet, in fact, was the only non-Virginian to hold a significant place in that army's high command for an extended period. He, therefore, outranked Early and all of the other Virginians (except Lee) in an army in which some 40–50 percent of the troops hailed from the Old Dominion.

Numerous writers have pointed out that Early's deep bitterness toward Longstreet may well have been motivated, at least in part, by a desire to divert attention from his own questionable conduct at Gettysburg, the Wilderness, Cedar Creek (the actual battle), and elsewhere.

(Early and many other former Confederates—some of whom disagreed with him about Longstreet—assumed as a matter of course that the East in general, and Virginia in particular, had constituted the crucial theater where the outcome of the war had been decided; that Gettysburg had been the battle that had determined that outcome; and

2. Foster, *Ghosts of the Confederacy: Defeat, The Lost Cause, and the Emergence of the New South* (New York: Oxford Univ. Press, 1987), 58–61.

that a Rebel victory there would have meant Confederate independence. As can be seen both from question 3 in the counterfactual section of the foreword and from the discussion of the "decisive battle" problem below, I disagree with all three of these assumptions.)

Even as the generation of Americans that had fought the war passed from the scene, professional historians gleefully took up the task of lengthening the list of reasons for Confederate defeat. Over the ensuing decades they have produced numerous learned tomes in which they have attributed the South's failure to establish its independent nationhood to one or more of a large group of factors.

The roster includes: moral qualms about the institution of slavery on the part of Southern whites; the moral superiority of the Union cause (an explanation very popular in the North in the decades immediately after the war); the increasing importance of Northern wheat relative to Southern cotton in the European market; desertions from the Rebel army; class resentment in the South at "a rich man's war and a poor man's fight"; failure of the Confederacy to win full diplomatic recognition from foreign governments—especially those of Great Britain and France (owing, some historians assert, to superior Northern diplomacy); a stronger devotion to the Union cause on the part of the common soldiers of the North relative to the Rebel soldiers' weaker allegiance to their cause; weak Confederate nationalism; adherence by the Southerners to the doctrine and practice of state (often erroneously "state's" or "states'") rights, which is said to have weakened the South's national war effort; inflexible political and military leadership in the Confederacy; failure of the secessionist government to stockpile cotton in Europe at the beginning of the war so as to be able to use it later as collateral for loans or to sell it to raise funds; low taxes (1 percent of income contrasted to 23 percent in the North); an excess of democracy or "democratic liberties" (even to the extent of electing the Rebel army's sergeants!); failure (or refusal) of the secessionists to curtail the cultivation of cotton and to replace that great staple crop with corn or other foodstuffs; the absence of organized political parties from the Confederacy's governmental structure; an excess of personal pride and arrogance ("big-man-me-ism") on the part of top Rebel political and military figures; the disaffection of the Confederacy's black population; the blockade of Southern ports by the Federal navy; the loss (or lack) of will to wage a prolonged struggle; inflation and the consequent depreciation of Confederate currency;[3] the secessionist government's neglect of the needs of the South's civilian population; malnutrition; Abraham Lincoln's superiority over Jefferson Davis as commander in chief; Davis's exaggerated opinion of his own military abilities; Davis's lack of political and/or human relations skills (or some other similar and equally glaring personal deficiency on the part of the Rebel chief executive); an exaggerated sense of individualism in the Confederacy; the lack of high-level administrative ability on the part of Confederate generals and politicians; religious doubts that led Southerners to think that God might not be on their side after all; Celtic military practices that led ("programmed," as it were) the Southerners to use their Celtic forebears' outmoded battlefield tactics in an age of modern weapons; Robert E. Lee's inability (owing to any one or more of several—mostly psychological—reasons) to adapt to the changed conditions of warfare in the 1860s; refusal by the secessionist government to curb civil liberties (freedom of the press, of speech, etc.), which permitted disloyal elements in the Confederacy to undermine the war effort; impressment of livestock, crops, and other goods, which generated great resentment against the Rebel government on the part of Southern civilians, especially those in the lower socioeconomic strata of Confederate society; the loss of Albert Sidney Johnston at Shiloh on April 6, 1862; the loss of "Stonewall" Jackson at Chancellorsville in May 1863; the breakdown of the Confederacy's system of transportation; and the disenchantment of Southern women at either their subordinate position in the patriarchal structure of the society in which they lived, or at the inability of the Rebel patriarchs to protect them from the dangers supposedly posed by the invading Yankees.

3. "One reason the South lost was that they made Confederate money, not knowing it was worthless." Quoted in Art Linkletter, *Kids Rite Funny: A Child's Garden of Misinformation* (N.p.: Bernard Geis Associates, 1962), 78.

At this juncture, any sane reader would be fully justified in throwing up his or her hands and demanding to know if historians can agree about any question of importance, or if they are like economists, of whom it is said that, if laid end to end, they would point in all directions.

Generally speaking, all of these attempts to account for the military outcome of the Civil War have two things in common. For one, almost all of them more-or-less accurately describe some facet of the conflict. After all, neither Great Britain nor France nor any other foreign government bestowed full diplomatic status on the Southern Confederacy; inflation, which by some measures reached 9,000 percent by the end of the war, did ravage the Rebel economy and hurt many Southerners—especially the poor; Jefferson Davis did not take much interest in the problems of those on the home front; and so on.

Second, none of these factors—nor even all of them taken together—can explain why the South lost the war. Some of the historians' reasons contradict each other. Many also applied to the North at least to the degree that they applied to the Confederacy. Most of them, in fact, reflect the *results* of Rebel defeat rather than having been factors that *caused* that defeat. A large number of them did not even begin to develop until sometime after the secessionists were already well along on the road to ultimate failure.

Some of these factors, we should note, did *affect* the nature of the war or of a particular campaign or engagement, but only in that they accelerated the Rebels' downfall, limited the Confederacy's ability to carry on a protracted struggle, or prevented the Rebels from reversing the tide of defeat that had already engulfed them—different matters entirely from their having led to or caused the defeat of secession.

The Union naval blockade of the Southern coast, for example, was ineffective in the early part of the war and never completely sealed off the Confederacy from the outside world. As its effectiveness increased over time, so did the Rebels' ability to manufacture domestically most of the weapons, ammunition, and other military items needed by their armies. Long before the blockade or the shortage of horses (or of anything else) began seriously to hamper the Southerners' military operations, the Rebels had already suffered the battlefield defeats that were to bring about their failure.

The western paradigm shows us at a glance the reason for Confederate defeat. The matter was brutally simple: The secessionists lost the war because their armies lost the key battles. As historian Gabor S. Boritt has noted of essentially the same assertion: "This statement is so self-evident as to make one who utters it look simpleminded. Yet many professional historians do not seem to grasp this simple truth." (I believe it would be more accurate to say "obviously do not grasp. . . .")

Many late-twentieth-century historians have demonstrated an unfortunate tendency to neglect military (and other traditional areas of) history and to flit off in pursuit of trendy new fields of inquiry. While many such new areas are legitimate, important, and should be fully explored and taken into consideration in our efforts to understand the past, it is a most serious mistake to discard older fields of inquiry simply because they are unfashionable at the moment. This observation is especially valid when the field being discarded is military history and the matter in question is why a war was won or lost. Writer Cyril Falls once observed, "It is remarkable how many people exert themselves and go through contortions to prove that battles and wars are won by any means except that by which they are most commonly won, which is by fighting."[4]

No Rebel army, furthermore, ever lost a battle because of inflation; or because the North had more boots; or because Great Britain, France, and China did not recognize the Confederacy as a sovereign nation; or because unhappy Southern women resented their subordinate position in their society; or for any of the other reasons listed above that do not relate directly to events on the battlefield. Even the relevance of many of those that do relate directly to the battles is subject to question.

Many of the defeats, we should note, came after the military outcome of the war had been decided; others stemmed from earlier lost

4. Boritt, *Why the Confederacy Lost* (New York: Oxford Univ. Press, 1992), 5; Falls quoted in T. Harry Williams, "The Military Leadership of North and South," in *Why the North Won the Civil War,* ed. David Donald (New York, Collier Books, 1962), 34.

battles. The losses suffered by the Rebels in Kentucky and Tennessee in the first months of 1862, for example, caused or exacerbated shortages of one thing or another. Those shortages, in turn, further weakened the Confederacy, led to suffering on the part of the Confederacy's civilians, and severely hampered the secessionist armies in the battles of 1863, 1864, and 1865.

When a Southern army lost a battle and consequently retreated and abandoned an area, the secessionists lost that area's resources, the economic and logistical burden on the remaining parts of Rebeldom increased, and refugees from the lost territory caused even more problems and suffering on the part of Confederate civilians. Had the secessionists won the early 1862 battles at Mill Springs and Fort Donelson, for example, they might have retained almost all of Tennessee and crucial parts of Kentucky along with the vast resources of those areas. They, therefore, would not have suffered such severe shortages later in the war. Retention of those areas for even a few months would have had some impact on the Confederacy's logistical capability to carry on the war in subsequent months or, perhaps, years.

Students of the war who ingested the old (eastern, or Virginia) paradigm with their mother's milk and their Pablum will immediately counter with a long list of battles won by the Rebels (see Part 4, note 5). Frequently, they will conclude their outburst with a paean to the great fighting prowess displayed by the hopelessly outnumbered, heroic, barefooted, starving, near-naked, virtually unarmed boys and old men in gray who rushed forth to fight for their country and who for four long years courageously defended their homes, families, and firesides, hurling back one massive horde of invading Yankees after another.

The secessionists did, in fact, manage to win an impressive number of battles. Virtually all of their successes, however, took place around the periphery of the conflict—along a line that ran from west to east from New Mexico to Florida and thence northward up the Atlantic Coast to Virginia. The long list includes Valverde, Palmetto Ranch, Sabine Pass, Fulton (Mo.), Wilson's Creek (Oak Hill, Springfield), Lexington (Mo.),

Mansfield (Sabine Cross Roads), Poison Spring, Marks' Mill, Brice's Cross Roads, Tupelo (Harrisburg), Natural Bridge (Fla.), Olustee, Honey Hill, Secessionville, Battery Wagner, Plymouth, Manassas (twice), Gaines's Mill, Fredericksburg, Chancellorsville, and Cold Harbor.

None of these engagements (nor any of the other Confederate victories) brought any lasting advantage to the Rebels. Other than boosting secessionist morale, sometimes temporarily depressing public support for the war effort in the North, enhancing (sometimes temporarily) the reputations of the victorious Southern generals, and—in some cases—postponing the end of the war for a brief time, all of these Confederate battlefield triumphs were, for all practical purposes, barren of significant results.

If then the secessionist armies won numerous victories but the Confederacy lost the war because the Rebel armies lost the key battles, we find ourselves dealing with a seeming paradox. In fact, however, this problem brings us face to face with the really important question: *Which* battles did the secessionists lose that brought about their defeat? The western paradigm gives us the answer.

The key to understanding the military history of the Civil War—at least so far as the matter of eventual Confederate defeat (or Federal victory) is concerned—lies in the course of the struggle for the region extending from the Appalachian Mountains on the east westward across the Mississippi Valley and from the Ohio River on the north to the Gulf of Mexico on the south (the area of Kentucky, Tennessee, Mississippi, Alabama, and Georgia). Americans of the 1860s usually referred to this vast area as "the West." Many modern historians now call it (in whole or in part) "the Confederate heartland."[5]

Rebel armies in the West began losing battles soon after the opening of the war and continued losing them right through to the very end of

5. Until midsummer 1863 the area for two hundred miles or so immediately west of the Mississippi River and stretching from the mouth of the Ohio on the north to the mouth of the Great River on the south constituted a corridor that should also be included in "the West." When the Yankees gained control of the entire length of the Mississippi in 1863, they sheared

the conflict. The history of Confederate arms in the West is the story of a virtually unbroken string of defeats, and those defeats determined the outcome of the war. (Or, the history of Federal arms in the West is the story of a virtually unbroken string of victories, and those victories determined the outcome of the war.) Only the Battle of Chickamauga (September 19–20, 1863) stands out as a major exception to the long catalogue of Confederate failures (or Union victories) in the West. Having won that terrible struggle at great cost (some eighteen thousand men), the Southerners proved unable to derive any advantage from their unaccustomed success.

Over the years numerous historians have pointed out that to secure their independence, the Confederates did not have to gain a military victory over the U.S. government. That is, the Rebels did not have to achieve the very difficult goals of conquering the North or of destroying the

---

that strip of land off from the Confederate West. By the end of 1864 "the West" had expanded to the east and included Savannah, Georgia. By the spring of 1865 it extended into northeastern North Carolina—a simple fact that in and of itself goes far to explain Confederate defeat.

In *A Great Civil War: A Military and Political History, 1861–1865* (Bloomington: Indiana Univ. Press, 2000), Russell F. Weigley argues that "the Washington-Richmond area was the crucial theater of [the] war" (93) and calls that region "the decisive Eastern theater of war" (136). Weigley bases this assertion on the claim that "the moral, political, and economic importance of the Confederate East" led Northerners to "the perception that a dramatic military victory in the East carried indeed the best promise of a short war" (60). The Virginia theater, therefore, "promise[d] a quick end to the entire contest" (108). " The Eastern theater . . . always held greater prospects and dangers for the immediate resolution of the war" (158). Weigley thus maintains that the East was the decisive theater because it offered the *potential* (my emphasis) for a quick victory for the North that would end the war, which was what the Northern public wanted.

I believe that Weigley's statements of fact are accurate but that they do not lead to his conclusion. Was being potentially the most important theater the same as being the most important theater? I think not.

After making the assertions described above, Weigley goes on for the better part of three hundred pages to narrate a history of battles and campaigns in which various Union generals in the East (including Ulysses S. Grant) failed to realize this potential. Meanwhile, Weigley's narrative shows, Federal armies in the West proceeded to dismember the Confederacy and make it impossible for the Rebels to continue the war in Virginia—or anywhere else.

I shall argue below that the East offered the Confederates their best chance to win their independence. They too, like the unionists, were not able to realize their goals in Virginia, and therefore the war in the East became a stalemate—a condition that favored the secessionists. Meanwhile, the Northern army and navy went about winning the war in the West. See also Parts 1, 2, and 3.

Union armies on the battlefield, although had they managed to accomplish either of those feats, they would have won the war. Instead of success through such improbable (probably impossible) military triumphs, the secessionists could achieve their goal of independence *if they could avoid defeat* and in so doing wear down their enemy and convince the people of the North that a victory for the national government would cost more than it would be worth. Northern voters would then turn the Lincoln administration out of office and replace it with a government willing to recognize the Confederacy as a sovereign nation.

Not losing thus became the key to winning for the secessionists. To succeed (and, therefore, to secede), however, the Southerners had to *avoid major defeats* in *both* of the main theaters of the war—East *and* West. For them, *to lose in either was to lose everything.* In Virginia the Rebels achieved their goal of not losing and, in fact, on several occasions came very close to demoralizing the Northerners (as the Bates diary entry quoted in Part 4 illustrates). While they were doing this, however, their equally brave and intelligent comrades in the West lost the battles that determined the military outcome of the war.

If secessionist troops could win battles and avoid defeat in Virginia, why did the Rebel armies in the West not enjoy a like success? Clearly, Confederate defeats in the West were not the result of James Longstreet's July 1863 conduct (or misconduct) at Gettysburg, although his fall 1863 performance at Chattanooga is a different matter. Nor were the lost western battles the products of "overwhelming numbers." In fact, the western Confederates outnumbered or were virtually equal in strength to their opponents in several crucial engagements (the opening stages of the struggle for Fort Donelson, Pea Ridge, the prelude to and the first day at Shiloh, Baton Rouge, Iuka, Corinth, Prairie Grove, the early part of the Vicksburg campaign, Milliken's Bend, Helena, Chickamauga, Peachtree Creek, Spring Hill, and Franklin). At Pea Ridge (March 7–8, 1862), for example, a Union force of about 10,500 defeated a 17,000-man Confederate army. We should also remember that the Rebels in Virginia won many of their victories despite being outnumbered.

Several regional factors—such as the area's relatively underdeveloped transportation and economic infrastructure—the sometimes counterproductive overall military policies of the Rebel government, and the general bumbling that often characterized the military activities of secessionist authorities all played some background role in the Confederacy's inability to win in the West. Two major reasons peculiar to the region, however, stand out above all others: its geography and the very poor quality of generalship consistently displayed by the Rebel commanders in the area. The former proved an especially severe handicap in the first two years of the conflict; the latter, however, quickly became the greater burden for the western Confederates and crippled them throughout the war. In truth, it greatly exacerbated the difficulties caused by geography and all the other factors.[6]

Three mighty rivers—the Mississippi, the Tennessee, and the Cumberland—opened up much of the western Confederacy to Union naval and land forces. The Rebels had neither a river navy of any note nor the facilities for constructing a meaningful number of formidable warships with which to defend these crucial waterways—especially after they lost New Orleans in late April 1862. Even worse for the Confederates, the three rivers did not connect with each other. To go from one to another, vessels had to use the Ohio River, which was under Yankee control throughout the war. This simple fact of geography meant that to mount a successful naval defense in the West, the secessionists would need three separate fleets (one on each river), each strong enough to meet the entire Union river fleet. The Rebels would also have needed a fourth such force to defend the mouth of the Mississippi against attacks from the Gulf of Mexico.

Even the few naval vessels the Southerners did manage to put afloat on the western waters proved, without exception, to be slow, clumsy, weak, underpowered, poorly armed, and unable to do more than occa-

6. See Richard M. McMurry, *Two Great Rebel Armies: An Essay in Confederate Military History* (Chapel Hill: Univ. of North Carolina Press, 1989).

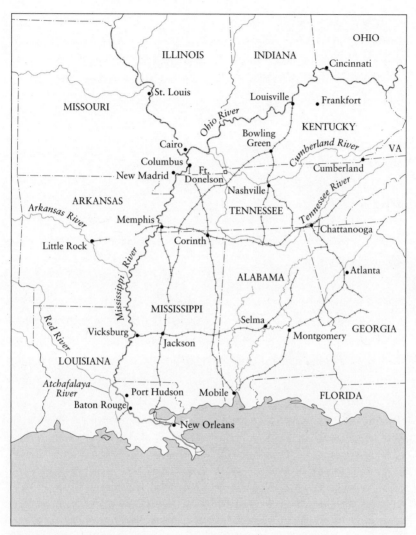

The Western theater, 1861–64.

sionally surprise and annoy the Federal government's large fleet of powerful river gunboats and rams as well as the great ocean-going warships that sometimes steamed up the Mississippi from the Gulf of Mexico. In summary, those three great rivers, along with several lesser streams in the West, offered secure lines of invasion, transportation, supply, and communication to the Yankees.

Control of the rivers in the West gave the unionists a degree of mobility that the Confederates could never match. Once patrolled by the Federal navy, the rivers themselves became major obstacles to the movement of Confederate armies and supplies. No sizable secessionist military force ever crossed the Mississippi or the lower stretches of the Tennessee or the Cumberland once Union gunboats gained access to those waterways.[7]

Incompetent Rebel generals compounded several times over the strategic difficulties that the western rivers posed for the secessionists, and they created a large number of other problems on their own.

Without a river navy of any consequence or the facilities for building one, the Confederates from the beginning of the war found themselves

---

7. Some writers have maintained that the Confederacy's great size gave the Rebels a geographic advantage since the Union forces would have to conquer so large an area. These commentators attempt to compare the Confederacy in this respect to Russia (or the Soviet Union), where the country's vast distances have swallowed up and frustrated invading armies for centuries. If, however, we discount the Trans-Mississippi (Texas, Arkansas, and Louisiana west of the Mississippi River), West Virginia, and Florida—all marginal areas from a Confederate military perspective—we can see that the Confederacy was not an especially large country. The eleven states of Rebeldom totaled 776,734 square miles. Of that total, 57 percent (442,002 square miles) was in the areas indicated above as not of significant military importance; 43 percent (334,732 square miles) was in states of significant military value. Even these numbers distort the picture since large portions of South Georgia, southeastern Alabama, western North Carolina, and southern Mississippi were of relatively little military worth. In fact, the militarily crucial part of the Confederacy was only about the size of Texas. The truth is that the Confederacy was not a country like Russia where defending armies could retreat into a vast interior for thousands of miles, where rivers did not offer invaders easy access to the interior of the country, and where a hostile navy did not hover offshore only two or three hundred miles (at most) from an invading army's starting point, thus offering that army a protected supply base and a secure place of refuge. Nor, we should note, was the Confederate winter anything like that with which armies invading Russia have had to contend.

compelled to rely primarily on riverside fortifications utilizing big cannon to close the navigable waterways to the invading Yankees. To defend the West the Rebels had to block the rivers at four key points: the lower Tennessee and the lower Cumberland Rivers to keep Yankee vessels out of Tennessee; the lower Mississippi to block the passage of Federal warships steaming upstream from the Gulf of Mexico; and the upper Mississippi to prevent Northern vessels from moving downriver through the center of the Confederacy.[8]

There simply were no good sites at which to construct land fortifications that might close the lower Tennessee and Mississippi Rivers. Early in 1862, Union naval vessels proved able to overpower Confederate installations on those two waterways without much trouble. Fort Henry, the Rebels' defensive work on the Tennessee, stood on such low ground that at the time it came under attack in February 1862 it had partly flooded. The crew of the Federal boat that came to receive the Confederate surrender simply rowed the little craft directly into the fort.[9]

8. "Upper" here is used from the Confederate point of view and refers to the stretch of the river flowing past the western side of Kentucky and Tennessee as far south as the Mississippi Delta, not to the part of the Mississippi above St. Louis to which the term is usually applied.

9. The terrain downriver (north) from Fort Henry, below Eddyville, was much more favorable for defense, but that and other such sites were in Kentucky, and the secessionists could not utilize them until the status of the Bluegrass State had been determined (see the section "That Elusive Turning Point" below). Nor could they have located Fort Henry farther upriver (south) in Tennessee without exposing nearby Fort Donelson on the Cumberland River to being outflanked, opening much of West Tennessee to the Federals and possibly—depending upon where they built their defenses—exposing the bridge that carried the crucial Memphis, Clarksville & Louisville Railroad over the Tennessee a short distance above the site where Fort Henry stood. The Rebels, therefore, had no choice but to put the installation on very bad ground. By the time they gained access to Kentucky, they had invested time, energy, and other resources in constructing Fort Henry, and the general confusion and incompetence that were to characterize the Confederate high command in the West had set in. The Rebel commanders concluded that they would be better off to continue work on Fort Henry. They did begin a sluggish effort to construct what would have become a much stronger installation (Fort Heiman) on high ground along the left bank of the river in Kentucky, but the work was not far advanced when the Yankees struck. See Thomas Lawrence Connelly, *Army of the Heartland: The Army of Tennessee, 1861–1862* (Baton Rouge: Louisiana State Univ. Press, 1967), 78–85; and Benjamin F. Cooling, *Forts Henry and Donelson: The Key to the Confederate Heartland* (Knoxville: Univ. of Tennessee Press, 1987), 46–62.

At Fort Donelson, which stood on high ground beside the Cumberland River, the Yankee army bottled up the Confederate garrison in the fort and its outer works. The Rebels made a surprise attack and drove back one wing of the Federal line, thereby opening an escape route. The secessionist generals then marched their men back into the fort to surrender. Before the capitulation, however, the two top Confederate commanders at Donelson, Brigadier Generals John B. Floyd and Gideon J. Pillow, fled from the scene, abandoning the troops to their fate. Floyd, a Virginia politician, did, nevertheless, make sure that his contingent of Virginia troops (and voters) got away from the fort by steamboat prior to the surrender.

In the summer of 1863 Lt. Gen. John C. Pemberton, commanding the Rebel troops defending Vicksburg, Mississippi, chose to ignore the orders of his superior officer, parked his men in the city's fortifications, and after a siege of seven weeks had to surrender them, the city, and all control of the river. At Island Number Ten, Arkansas Post, and Port Hudson, thousands of other Southerners suffered the same fate for the same basic reason.

In all, the Confederates' unsuccessful 1862–63 efforts to hold these river posts cost the South more than sixty thousand men surrendered as prisoners of war and at least twenty thousand more killed, wounded, captured, or lost to disease in the sieges and in the battles leading up to the sieges. In every one of these instances, the Rebel commanders *chose* the course of action or inaction that led directly to the surrender of their garrisons (although, in their defense, we should point out that many of them were simply doing what they thought their government wished them to do—hold their posts as long as possible).

The cases of Vicksburg and Port Hudson illustrate perhaps better than any others the chaos, confusion, and incompetence that characterized so much of the Confederate war effort in the West. (See also "The Search for the Decisive Battle" below.) By the summer of 1862 the two positions marked the upper (northern) and lower (southern) limits of the short stretch of the Mississippi River that then remained under Confederate control. Unless they could keep Yankee gunboats out of the section of the river between Vicksburg and Port Hudson, the secessionists would lose communication between the eastern and western halves of their country. Once by the Rebel fortifications at *either* point, Union vessels could reach and block the mouth of the Red River and, for all practical purposes, make it impossible for the Southerners to move supplies, food, and large bodies of troops or animals back and forth across the Mississippi.

Unfortunately for the Rebels, the Yankees also had a third route by which they could reach the lower Red River. Union forces could move west from occupied New Orleans and then up Bayou Teche and the Atchafalaya River to enter the Red River. Federal success along any of these three routes would cut Rebeldom in two.

Confederate defenses along the Mississippi were especially confused in the spring of 1863. The region west of the Great River had just passed under the command of Lt. Gen. Edmund Kirby Smith, whose troops were scattered throughout Arkansas, Louisiana, and Texas. The area east of the Mississippi was under the command of Gen. Joseph E. Johnston, who was then both ill and absorbed by problems in the Tennessee sector of his command. Direct responsibility for the defense of Mississippi rested on the shoulders of Johnston's subordinate Pemberton. Neither Johnston nor Smith was subject to any command other than that of the president and the War Department in distant Richmond.

To confuse matters even more, Confederate authorities in Richmond—usually President Davis himself, whose home was on the Mississippi a short distance south of Vicksburg—both refused to give Smith and Johnston any meaningful guidance as to broad objectives or priorities and often issued orders or made suggestions directly to Pemberton (which he interpreted as orders) without coordinating with Johnston or even informing him as to what they had done. Johnston, meanwhile, convinced himself that the secessionist forces in Mississippi should be separated from his command and united with the Trans-Mississippi troops under the authority of Smith.

Apparently, no one thought to ask what should be done in the event the Yankees crossed to the west side of the Mississippi (Smith's area) to

operate against Vicksburg (Johnston and Pemberton's area), thus splitting the seam of the Confederate defenses in the Mississippi Valley. The
point at which two independent commands join is always a weak spot. In
this case, weakness was compounded by all the other factors that so hampered the Rebels. With so many people managing parts of the Confederate effort in the area, no one had overall responsibility. The whole arrangement was a disaster waiting to happen—in the spring of 1863 it did.

On the night of April 16–17, Federal gunboats managed to run downstream past the Vicksburg batteries. Their presence in the river between
Vicksburg and Port Hudson rendered Rebel retention of the two towns
meaningless. Much the same thing happened at about the same time on
the lower Mississippi River when the unionists advancing from New
Orleans easily took control of Bayou Teche and the Atchafalaya River,
thereby gaining access to the lower Red River. Northern gunboats and
troops were therefore able to sever the secessionists' Red River line of
communication as of mid-April 1863.[10]

A month after the Yankees achieved this success, Pemberton—acting under what he understood to be President Davis's directive but dis-
obeying instructions he received from Johnston—shut his armies up in
Vicksburg and Port Hudson in a hopeless effort to protect a line of communication that the Confederates had lost four weeks earlier. Afterward,
Davis expected Johnston to organize an army in east-central Mississippi
to relieve Pemberton. Johnston, however, believed that such an effort
was hopeless, which, in fact, it was. By holding the two river towns after
mid-April, the Rebels did temporarily deny Northern merchant boats
use of the Mississippi, but that was scant compensation for the troops
tied up in and eventually surrendered with the towns.

---

10. Command of the Federal forces in the Mississippi Valley was also divided, but the division was between forces operating south from Memphis and those moving north from New
Orleans. This arrangement worked, though, because it gave each commander authority over
operations on both sides of the Mississippi River and was necessitated by the distance that
separated the two columns and the presence of a major Confederate force between them.
Many thanks to Bill Shea for calling this point to my attention.

Meanwhile, many other Confederate generals elsewhere in the West kept busy demonstrating their propensity to disobey orders, a wide streak of battlefield incompetence, and a tendency to quarrel among themselves to such a debilitating extent that they severely weakened their own army's capability to defend the region of the Confederacy entrusted to its care. The worst by far of these offenders, at least in terms of the overall damage he did to the secessionist cause, was Leonidas Polk, who at the beginning of the war held the post of Episcopal bishop of Louisiana.

In the summer of 1861 President Jefferson Davis appointed his old friend Polk a major general and assigned him to command Confederate forces on the upper Mississippi. Polk was an alumnus of the U.S. Military Academy, where he and Davis had met and become friends, but he had resigned from the army to enter the ministry almost immediately after his 1827 graduation (Davis had graduated with the Class of 1828).

Polk's early appointment as a major general and subsequent promotion to lieutenant general made him one of the highest-ranking officers in the secessionist army. In fact, only Rebel full generals and one lieutenant general were senior to him. For much of the war he stood second in rank among Confederate generals in the West.

During the brief period in the late summer of 1861, when Polk exercised independent command on the upper Mississippi, he *chose* to disobey Davis's standing instructions by violating the "neutrality" that Kentucky was then seeking to maintain between the warring sections. In so doing, Polk pushed the crucial Bluegrass State into the arms of the Federal government. His reckless act gained nothing of importance for the Rebels, and, in fact, it brought almost immediate disaster to the Confederacy. (This is more fully discussed in "That Elusive Turning Point" below.)

Later, after Gen. Braxton Bragg had taken command of the Confederates' principal western army in June 1862, Polk became his highest-ranking subordinate. For the next sixteen months, Polk devoted much of his time, energy, and considerable influence to mostly successful efforts to undermine Bragg. Polk led an anti-Bragg cabal consisting of many of the army's generals and worked assiduously to erode his commander's influence with the officers and men. Those efforts on the bishop's part stirred up a miniature civil war within the army. On several crucial occasions Polk chose to disobey Bragg's battlefield orders.

Polk's prestige as a high-ranking clergyman, his political connections, and his long friendship with Jefferson Davis shielded him from the trial by court-martial that his conduct fully merited. His detrimental and divisive influence on the western Confederate army lingered on even after June 14, 1864, when a Yankee cannonball put a stop to the immediate harm that he was doing.

Although worse and far more damaging to the Confederate cause than the behavior of other secessionist generals, Polk's irresponsible conduct was not unique. A good many of Polk's fellow western commanders demonstrated their own misconduct and lack of competence on numerous occasions throughout the war. On September 10, 1863, for example, Bragg planned an attack on an isolated Union force in the cul-de-sac of McLemore's Cove in northwestern Georgia. Lt. Gen. Daniel Harvey Hill decided not to obey Bragg's orders to join the assault. Perhaps it was just as well because Maj. Gen. Thomas C. Hindman, commanding another attacking column, had meanwhile decided on his own not to launch the assault Bragg had ordered him to make in conjunction with Hill's attack. Maj. Gen. Simon B. Buckner, sent to reinforce Hindman, joined the latter in deciding to do nothing. The next day found the Yankees gone from the trap.

Ten months later at Peachtree Creek just north of Atlanta, Lt. Gen. William J. Hardee, commanding the Rebel forces on the field, could manage to get only two of his seven infantry divisions seriously engaged in the battle. Two days after the defeat at Peachtree Creek, Hardee again wasted his troops in piecemeal attacks during the Battle of Atlanta. In 1862 and 1863 Hardee had been Polk's chief accomplice in the latter's unceasing vendetta against Bragg; in July and August 1864 he was to prove uncooperative with his new commander, Gen. John Bell Hood, whose promotion he resented.

The western Confederate generals saved what proved to be their best (or worst) display of foolishness and incompetence for the night of

November 29–30, 1864. On the twenty-ninth, Southern troops made a heroic march to position themselves in fields a short distance east of the road between Columbia and Spring Hill, Tennessee, and just south of the latter town. If the Rebels had moved west a short distance and blocked the road or had they gone north to seize the town, they might have been able to cut off a Union column then marching northward along the road in an effort to reach safety in Nashville.

Owing to their generals' many (still unexplained) failures, the troops remained all night just off the road while the Yankees tramped past their camps and escaped. Stories (possibly apocryphal) have come down through the years telling of Northern soldiers actually leaving their marching column and stopping to light their pipes and cigars at the Confederates' campfires. One Rebel private, alarmed at what he saw happening, even went to the nearby plantation house where the army commander had made his headquarters, awakened him, and reported that the enemy was escaping the trap. That general then ordered a staff officer to instruct one of the corps commanders to send troops to block the road. The staff officer later said that he was so exhausted that he fell asleep without sending the message. The corps commander later reported that when he received the order that the staff officer said he did not send, he immediately sent troops to check the road. When the troops reached the road, they found it deserted and returned to their camps. In summary, the Confederate generals simply could not get themselves organized enough that night to do anything effectively.

When he awakened on the morning of November 30, a furious Gen. John Bell Hood, commanding the secessionist army, blamed just about everybody in the army but himself for the fiasco. In truth, Hood was probably more at fault than anyone since the basic cause of the problem seems to have stemmed from conflicting orders that he apparently gave to a corps commander and (separately) directly to a division commander, thus violating the chain of command and setting his two subordinates to working at cross purposes. After sowing the seeds of the mess, Hood then left the field and retired to the plantation house where he established his headquarters for the night. (Some reports state that he and/or several subordinates and staff officers then engaged in too much drinking.) On the afternoon of the thirtieth, an angry and frustrated Hood hurled his men against the Federals, who by then had taken up a very strong position at Franklin, north of Spring Hill. The Rebel troops were slaughtered.

To be sure, the Confederates might well have lost the western battles and campaigns even had their generals charged with defending the area acted with great wisdom, self-discipline, professionalism, and brilliance— or even basic competence. After all, the Rebels did face a strong, adequately supplied, well-led, confident foe, and they suffered from many serious disadvantages in the region that had nothing to do with their generals. As it was, however, their loss of the West clearly came about *as soon as* it did as the direct result of the bad conduct, wretched personalities, shortsightedness, and outright incompetence (often bordering on the criminal) of the generals who directed Confederate armies in that area. Those officers managed to turn what were probably unavoidable defeats—that could, however, almost certainly have been postponed for months if not for a year or two—into major and irredeemable disasters that occurred much earlier than otherwise would have been the case.

Would better generals have enabled the secessionists to hold the West? It seems most unlikely given the great geographic and other disadvantages the Rebels faced there, especially in the area north of the Tennessee River. Certainly, however, a more competent set of commanders could have delayed the Union conquest of the western Confederacy, inflicted far more casualties on the invading Yankee armies, and saved tens of thousands of their own men who were lost to their generals' incompetence. In accomplishing all those goals, better Rebel commanders would have helped the South hold out longer and thereby have a chance to win by not losing.

Some 14,000 Confederates were shipped off to prisoner of war camps in the North after Fort Donelson surrendered in February 1862. Had those men taken part in the Battle of Shiloh seven weeks later, that great and bloody struggle might well have had a different outcome. Had even half of the 35,000 secessionist troops who surrendered at Vicksburg and Port Hudson in July 1863 served in the fighting ranks at Chickamauga the following September, even the western Confederate generals might have been able to make something out of the costly victory their army won for them on that terrible battlefield.

In summary, the Confederacy lost the war because the Confederate armies lost the great battles fought in the crucial area from the Appalachian Mountains westward to and across the Mississippi Valley. (Or, conversely, the Federals won the war because the Federal armies won the great battles fought in the crucial area from the Appalachian Mountains westward to and across the Mississippi Valley.) Although several other factors played roles of greater or lesser importance from time to time, the key ingredient in the Rebel defeats in the West and the conversion of those defeats into national disasters was incompetent generalship, especially at the army and corps command levels. Those defeats and disasters, in turn, were the reasons why the Confederacy failed to win its independence.

Historian Steven E. Woodworth has observed: "the weakness of the Confederacy's western defenses meant there could be no margin for error. Every blunder by an inept general would have disastrous effects."[11] In the West there were many inept Southern generals, and they made many serious blunders—most of which sooner rather than later turned into the military disasters that led directly to Rebel defeat.

The Search for the Decisive Battle

A second topic much debated among students of Civil War military history revolves around the matter of a (or *the*) "decisive battle." As with the annual American ritual of arguing over "the Number 1 team," much of the disagreement and fireworks arising from the question stem from the failure of most of those who seek "the decisive battle" to define what they mean by the term.

11. Woodworth, *Jefferson Davis and His Generals: The Failure of Confederate Command in the West* (Lawrence: Univ. Press of Kansas, 1990), 70. On the general subject of Confederate disadvantages/Union advantages in the West, see McMurry, *Two Great Rebel Armies.*

When applied to battlefield events, the adjective "decisive" can have meaning on four different levels. In the local or limited sense, one can use the word to designate a battle in which the victorious army gains a clear-cut (as opposed to an ambiguous) triumph on the field. To put it another way, after such a battle, there simply is no doubt as to which army can claim the victory. Such an engagement itself, however, may be of little— or even of no—consequence in the larger history of the war; the battle's results are pretty much limited to the field on which it took place. The engagement at Honey Hill, fought near Savannah, Georgia, on November 30, 1864, was an unambiguous—"decisive"—Rebel triumph in this sense. The Union force that had advanced inland from the South Carolina coast in an effort to cut the railroad between Savannah and Charleston suffered a clear defeat and withdrew from the field, leaving the rail line intact. The little battle, however, had no impact on the war or even on the campaign (the March to the Sea) of which it was a part.

On the second level the word "decisive" may be used to describe a battle that did determine the outcome of a campaign and was thus conclusive in that limited sense. The fight at Gaines's Mill on June 27, 1862, for example, decided the outcome of the Peninsular campaign. Gaines's Mill was also one of the most "important" battles of the war because the Rebel success in the Peninsular campaign preserved the balance in Virginia that otherwise almost certainly would have tilted to the Federals. On an even higher plane, the Confederate victory at Gaines's Mill and the continuing strategic stalemate in Virginia served indirectly to strengthen the hand of those in the North who argued that more severe ("radical") policies such as emancipation were necessary for the Union to triumph over the secessionists. (Would this fact make Robert E. Lee—or Brig. Gen. John Bell Hood, who led the final Confederate attack in the battle— the "Great Emancipator"?) None of these results, however, means that the battle was "decisive" in determining the military outcome of the North-South conflict.

Many of those who apply the word "decisive" to a Civil War engagement use the term on a third and higher level. They intend it to describe a battle that directly affected the military outcome of the war in some way—

usually by altering the direction in which its overall course was evolving. (This is further discussed in "That Elusive Turning Point" below.)

On the fourth and highest level, those who apply the term in this sense do so to designate *the* battle that they believe decided the outcome of the conflict or at least put the war irrevocably on the course that led ultimately to the Confederate surrender. It is in this last sense that I apply the term here.

Over the decades much—almost certainly most—of the attention and energy devoted to the search for the decisive battle of the American Civil War has focused on the great engagement that raged across the area around Gettysburg, Pennsylvania, during the course of the first three days of July 1863. In fact, the Battle of Gettysburg, while a clear victory for the Federal army and the engagement that determined the outcome of the campaign of which it was a part, was not a battle that altered the overall course of the war in any significant way, and it certainly did not settle the final outcome of the struggle. In the twenty-one months after Gettysburg, the conflict simply continued moving along the lines that had marked its earlier history and that were to characterize it until its end.

The great struggle in southern Pennsylvania was, to be sure, the war's largest single battle as measured by the number of casualties, but it owes its prominence in the literature of the war and in both the popular and scholarly mind to the fact that it was the only large battle fought on the soil of a free state; to the proximity of the battlefield to the great population, political, and press centers of the North; to President Abraham Lincoln's "Gettysburg Address"; and to several other factors, none of which has anything to do with the battle's place in the military annals of the war.

Most of the very little effort that has been devoted to assessing Gettysburg's impact on the course of the war—as opposed to asserting on faith the belief that it was "decisive"—has been conducted on a very superficial, almost journalistic, level. Can anyone point to a single military result of Gettysburg that had any impact beyond the campaign of which the engagement was a part? Can anyone discern a single way in which the overall military course of the war was different in the months after Gettysburg that had anything to do with the great battle?

The struggle at Gettysburg, in fact, has had a far greater impact on the tourist business in Adams County, Pennsylvania, than it ever had on the military outcome of the Civil War. As one modern historian has commented, the battle made Gettysburg "a town where the dead support the living."[12]

By one count, 2,261 military engagements of one sort or another took place during the Civil War.[13] Doubtless eventually we shall have at least one book, doctoral dissertation, journal article, master's thesis, or college term paper written about every one of them, and the author of each of those studies will argue passionately that his or her battle was "*the* decisive" contest that settled the final military outcome of the war and thereby sealed the fate of the Southern Confederacy.

More years ago now than I care to remember, a college senior wrote an eighty-something-page term paper for a Civil War and Reconstruction course. In that (possibly padded) work he asserted, with all the expertise and self-confidence of a twenty-one-year-old college senior, that *the* decisive engagement of the war had taken place on March 28, 1862,

12. James I. Robertson Jr., conversations with author. See Richard M. McMurry, "The Pennsylvania Gambit and the Gettysburg Splash," in *The Gettysburg Nobody Knows,* ed. Gabor S. Boritt (New York: Oxford Univ. Press, 1997), 175–202. A friend in the Civil War business who arranges tours and conferences has said, "*Of course* the western battles were more important, but people will *pay* to go to Gettysburg!" P. T. Barnum, it seems, was right after all. There *is* a sucker born every minute.

Some who study the war in the East, of course, realize that *something* happened west of the Alleghenies but choose, for reasons of their own, to pay no attention to events in that region. Instead, they immerse themselves in the eastern battles and campaigns and become experts on, say, the struggle that took place along the left of the line held by Company C, 20th Maine Infantry Regiment, between 2:17 and 3:09 P.M., July 2, 1863, on the western slope of Little Round Top south of Gettysburg. So long as these experts on this rather narrow topic do not attempt to pass themselves off as experts on the Civil War, they do no harm. The real danger comes when they extrapolate from their limited area of expertise to larger topics such as why the North won the war.

13. Frederick Phisterer, *Statistical Record of the Armies of the United States* (1883; reprint, Wilmington, N.C.: Broadfoot, 1989), 83–212.

at Pigeon Ranch in what is now New Mexico. When the invading Rebel force was compelled to retreat back down the Rio Grande into Texas, his argument went, the secessionists lost their chance to seize an unblockadable port on the Pacific through which supplies in unlimited quantities could have flowed to the hard-pressed Confederate armies in Tennessee, Mississippi, and Virginia. Fortunately, the instructor had a sense of humor.

In the quest for the decisive battle, as with the question of how (or why) the war ended in Confederate defeat (or Union victory), the western paradigm can provide an—if not *the*—answer.

If the eastern battles between the Army of Northern Virginia and the Army of the Potomac were bloody engagements that produced only a military stalemate, then by definition the battle or battles that brought about ultimate Federal victory could not have taken place in the Virginia theater. Those who accept the framework of the western paradigm can thus strike Gettysburg and all the other eastern battles from the list of possible decisive engagements. The same observation holds true for the clashes that took place in the Trans-Mississippi and along the coast of Rebeldom on the margins of the conflict. Since the Union won the war, no battle in which the Confederates were victorious could have been decisive in the sense in which we use the word here.

Once we have thus eliminated Rebel victories and the engagements that took place outside the West, we are positioned to examine the candidates that may have a legitimate claim to the title.

In 1960 Charles L. Dufour concluded that the war had been decided when it was just a little more than a year old. In *The Night the War Was Lost* he pointed to the moonless midnight blackness of April 23–24, 1862, as the time and to the lower Mississippi River as the place when and where the outcome of the conflict had been settled. That night Flag Officer David G. Farragut managed to run a dozen or so of the U.S. Navy's powerful ocean-going, steam-powered warships upriver past the Confederate guns in Forts Jackson and St. Philip some seventy miles below New Orleans. Once by the forts Farragut's fleet had the Confederacy's greatest metropolis at its mercy. When the Yankees occupied New Orleans a few days later, wrote Dufour, the Confederacy suffered a mortal blow.

Four years prior to the appearance of Dufour's book, Stanley F. Horn, one of the first historians to appreciate the key role of the western military operations, thought that he had spotted the war's most crucial engagement and that it had been fought just a few months prior to the end of the conflict. In *The Decisive Battle of Nashville* Horn argued that the clash outside Tennessee's capital city on December 15–16, 1864, had sealed the fate of the Confederacy. Once the remnants of the Rebel army had fled southward from Middle Tennessee, Horn maintained, Federal victory in the war was assured beyond all question. Had the secessionists won at Nashville, he asserted, "the whole aspect of the military situation would have changed."[14]

Undoubtedly, many students of the war will take issue with Dufour and/or Horn both as to the engagements they chose to label "decisive" and to the criteria they used in making their selections. Horn's choice, at least in part, is obviously based on speculation about what could have happened if the Confederates had won the Battle of Nashville—a different matter entirely from the actual results produced by the engagement itself (a set of negative, or counterfactual, rather than positive criteria for "decisiveness" as it were). Using this method any historian worth his or her salt can easily construct a logical argument that any one of the war's 2,261 battles was *the* decisive one—even Pigeon Ranch. Dufour and Horn, however, were clearly on the right track when they looked to the West to find the war's most important military engagement, though the author of the Pigeon Ranch study appears to have gone too far west.

If one insists on designating a single battle as *the* "decisive" one, my nominee for the honor is the relatively little-known action fought on May 16, 1863, on and around Champion Hill (often erroneously called

---

14. Horn, *The Decisive Battle of Nashville* (Baton Rouge: Louisiana State Univ. Press, 1956), vii–viii, xiii. See also John Fiske, *The Mississippi Valley in the Civil War* (Boston: Houghton Mifflin, 1900), for a strong and even earlier argument that the western theater is the key to understanding Civil War military history.

"Champion's Hill") in west-central Mississippi about halfway between Jackson and Vicksburg.

The Battle of Champion Hill enjoys the advantage of having both positive and negative criteria to support its claim, and both sets of criteria are clear cut. The battle proved crucial in terms of both the results that flowed from it and for what might well have happened had it been won by the Confederates. In all probability, a great ("decisive") Rebel victory at Champion Hill would have brought Ulysses S. Grant's Vicksburg campaign to an inglorious end and resulted in removal from command and disgrace for Grant himself even had he managed to avoid becoming a casualty in the battle. In fact, he might really have wound up chasing the Sioux in Minnesota or sitting idly in exile on the porch of his home in Galena, Illinois, drinking coffee or something stronger, munching vinegar-soaked cucumbers, and smoking cigars.

Under such circumstances Grant's senior subordinate in the Vicksburg campaign, Maj. Gen. John A. McClernand, would have become commander of the Union forces in the area—assuming that he survived the Federal debacle at Champion Hill. (See question 2 in the counterfactual section of the foreword.) Major Generals William T. Sherman and James B. McPherson, the other leading subordinates then with Grant's army, could have been killed, disabled by wounds, captured, fallen into disgrace along with the defeated Grant, or passed under McClernand's authority. None of these possible outcomes would have benefited the Union cause in the slightest. All of them, in fact, would have been very detrimental to it.

As it was, Grant's victory at Champion Hill made inevitable his capture of Vicksburg, the fall of Port Hudson, the reestablishment of Federal authority along the entire length of the Mississippi River, and the consequent splitting of the Confederacy. Given the mind-set of his opponent, Lt. Gen. John C. Pemberton, it also made inevitable the capture of the Confederate armies defending Vicksburg and Port Hudson. (Believing that President Davis wanted him to hold the two towns as long as possible, Pemberton shut up his troops in Vicksburg's massive fortifications to await relief by a Confederate army from the outside. He instructed the force at Port Hudson to hold that place until help came. The Rebels had to organize a relieving army virtually from scratch. Although they managed eventually to scrape together a small force, it was never very strong and failed utterly in its effort to save Vicksburg, Port Hudson, and their garrisons.)

These developments, in turn, freed Grant's mighty Army of the Tennessee, which had been campaigning in the Mississippi Valley, for subsequent operations along the even more crucial Nashville-Chattanooga-Atlanta corridor (the "backbone of the Confederacy"). They also cemented the people of the Old Northwest once and for all to the national cause by guaranteeing to them a commercial outlet down the Mississippi River. Last, but not least, success at Vicksburg made Grant in the popular mind what he already was in fact—by far the best of the Northern army commanders. Grant's subsequent elevation to the command of all Union forces in the West, the great November 1863 national victories at Chattanooga, and finally Grant's early 1864 promotion to command all Federal land forces flowed directly from the Battle of Champion Hill. No other single Civil War engagement produced so many and such important, far-reaching, and lasting results for the unionists.

For the Confederates, conversely, the road from Champion Hill led deep into disaster. The Rebels soon lost Vicksburg, Port Hudson, and control of the Mississippi River. They also suffered at least fifty thousand casualties in their unsuccessful effort to hold Vicksburg and Port Hudson. In July 1863, when these long campaigns ended, the Southerners found their country sliced in half by hostile forces, and many of the Rebels suffered great demoralization as a result. President Jefferson Davis and his numerous political and military critics fell into even more bitter, debilitating quarrels about secessionist policies, strategy, and the question of who was to blame for the loss of Vicksburg and the Mississippi Valley.

Those who fault James Longstreet for his alleged bad conduct at Gettysburg and, at least by implication, ascribe Confederate defeat both on that field and in the war to his activities (or inactivity) in that battle should take the time to examine the role played by Maj. Gen. William W. Loring at Champion Hill. Loring's behavior on that occasion stands as perhaps the most egregious example of willful misconduct on the part of a senior American military commander in any of the country's wars—with the possible exception of Benedict Arnold's treason—and Arnold, we should remember, had at least played a heroic, honorable, and crucial role in the important 1777 victory at Saratoga before he turned traitor. His treason, furthermore, did not take place on the battlefield in the face of the enemy.

On May 3, 1863, Loring with some 17,000 men had a chance to fall on the 11,000 Yankees of the Seventeenth Corps near Hankinson's Ferry on the Big Black River south of Vicksburg. He did nothing to take advantage of the opportunity. On the thirteenth, three days before the clash at Champion Hill, Loring found himself in command of some 22,000 Confederate troops posted on the left (eastern) side of the Big Black River between Vicksburg and Champion Hill. That day he missed a golden opportunity to pounce on the 13,000 Yankees of the Thirteenth Corps, who were then isolated in his immediate front.

Three days later Loring commanded the division of the Rebel army assigned to hold the right of the Confederate position at Champion Hill. Loring seethed with hatred for and contempt toward his commander, Lt. Gen. John C. Pemberton. He and members of his staff openly expressed their disdain for him—sometimes in the presence of subordinates. On occasion Loring did not trouble himself enough to pass important information along to his commander. One Confederate officer noted, "Loring would be willing for Pemberton to lose a battle provided that he would be displaced."[15] Some of the army's other senior officers, notably Brig. Gen. John S. Bowen, shared Loring's contempt for their commander. (One of the major problems seems to have been that Pemberton almost always rejected Loring's proposals to deal with the Yankees in their front.)

About 1:00 P.M. on May 16, Loring disobeyed an order from Pemberton to attack the Federals from his position on the right of the Southern line at Champion Hill. An hour or so later he disobeyed another order from

15. Quoted in Edwin C. Bearss, *The Campaign for Vicksburg*, 3 vols. (Dayton, Ohio: Morningside, 1985), 2:620.

Pemberton to reinforce the left of the Rebel army, which was then engaged in the crucial part of the battle. In both of these instances, we should note, Loring may well have been correct in the decisions he made—as Longstreet may well have been correct in his appraisal of the tactical situation at Gettysburg.

When Loring did eventually move to bolster the left of the Confederate line, he took a lengthy, obscure backcountry road without notifying his commander of his route, and Pemberton lost track of his division. Without Loring's reinforcements the Rebel commander soon ordered his army to retreat. When he finally located Loring, Pemberton directed him to cover the secessionists' withdrawal. Sometime later Loring concluded that he had been cut off from the rear of the army and that he should march off to the south and east—which he proceeded to do without sending word of his action to Pemberton.

As was the case with Leonidas Polk, Loring's baleful influence lingered on in the army even after he had left the scene. Following their defeat at Champion Hill, the surviving secessionists in Pemberton's force retreated west toward Vicksburg. On May 17 they tried to hold an indefensible position at the Big Black River to keep open a route of escape for Loring's missing division, which they naturally assumed was following the rest of the army. While Loring continued his march away from Pemberton's force, the unfortunate Rebels at the Big Black suffered yet another total, crushing defeat, and the ones who could get away fled into the trap of the Vicksburg fortifications.

Loring's bad conduct at Champion Hill was nothing new. Earlier, in the winter of 1861–62, when he was a brigadier general, Loring had openly been very critical of his commander ("Stonewall" Jackson in that instance) and had played a key role in undermining an effort by the Confederates to hold what is now northeastern West Virginia. Soon thereafter the Rebel government had promoted him to major general and sent him to the West.

Is the concept of a single "decisive" battle even a valid idea? I believe that, at least in the case of the American Civil War, it makes much more sense to think in terms of decisive campaigns or operations rather than in terms of one all-important battle. Certainly this observation applies to the western theater of the conflict. Four great campaigns determined the course of the war in the West, and as it turned out, the outcome of the conflict itself. Other than the fact that the later ones flowed naturally from those that had taken place earlier, there is no meaningful way to rank any one of them as "more decisive" or important than any of the others. In chronological order they were:

1. The Mill Springs–Fort Henry–Fort Donelson–Pea Ridge–Shiloh–Island Number Ten operations of early 1862, which broke the great Rebel defensive line across southern Kentucky and Missouri and resulted in the reestablishment of Federal authority over those two states as well as over much of West and Middle Tennessee and northeastern Arkansas. These operations also cost the secessionists Memphis, Nashville, New Orleans, and Pensacola (the Rebels stripped the last two points of troops to reinforce their army at Shiloh, and both soon fell to the Yankees); their one true east-west railroad; and at least 35,000 men. These campaigns also demoralized many Southerners and touched off much intramural bickering among the Rebels, especially between the Davis administration and its political opponents.[16]

2. The Vicksburg campaign of late 1862 and the first half of 1863, which, along with its ancillary operations (including Arkansas Post, Port Hudson, and the Union successes along Bayou Teche and the Atchafalaya River in the spring of 1863) cost the Southerners the Mississippi River, split the Confederacy in half, demoralized the secessionists even more, generated additional and even more bitter squabbles among the Rebel leaders, and resulted in more than 50,000 casualties in the Southern armies involved in these operations.

16. Historian Bell I. Wiley maintained that the great discord among the Confederates resulting from these disasters—especially the loss of Forts Henry and Donelson—made them *the* decisive military events of the war. Wiley, conversations with author. See also Wiley, *The Road to Appomattox* (Memphis: Memphis State College Press, 1956).

3. The Tullahoma-Chickamauga-Chattanooga-Knoxville operations in the late summer and fall of 1863, which cost the Rebels virtually all the rest of Tennessee and some 30,000 casualties, further demoralized the secessionists and set the stage for the last great operation that was to ensure Union victory beyond all doubt.

4. The Atlanta campaign of 1864, which among other things provided the battlefield success that assured the reelection of Abraham Lincoln and in so doing guaranteed that the Federal government would see the war through to final and absolute military victory rather than accept some compromise with secession and slavery. The campaign also resulted in the destruction of a key Confederate industrial and transportation center and cost the secessionists another 35,000 men. (Civil War buffs can argue the question of *when* the military events of the Atlanta campaign assured Lincoln's victory in the election. The fall of the city in early September—some two months prior to the election—was an obvious indication of Union success, but I believe that the crucial date—the last day on which the Confederacy had a reasonable chance to gain its independence—was May 8, when Yankee troops seized the unobstructed, unfortified, unguarded, and unobserved Snake Creek Gap in Rocky Face Ridge near Resaca. Once that crucial passage through the mountains of northwestern Georgia fell into Federal hands, the Yankees had an advantageous position that would enable them easily to flank the Rebels out of all of North Georgia. Historian Larry J. Daniel has argued, convincingly it seems to me, that such a Union success would have brought about Lincoln's reelection—although almost certainly by a smaller majority—even had Atlanta not fallen when it did.)[17]

Each of these four campaigns brought important *and* lasting changes in the military situation. Each produced *results*. After each of them any

17. Daniel, "The South Almost Won by Not Losing: A Rebuttal," *North & South* 1.3 (Feb. 1999): 44–51. See also Richard M. McMurry, *Atlanta 1864: Last Chance for the Confederacy* (Lincoln: Univ. of Nebraska Press, 2000), especially chap. 5.

observer could clearly see that the Rebels' overall plight was much worse than it had been when the campaign opened. Each took place in the West. In each of them bad Rebel generalship was the key factor, both in bringing about battlefield defeats for the Confederates and in ensuring that those defeats would quickly turn into major, irredeemable disasters.

During the war the secessionists more than held their own in Virginia. President Davis, however, could never bring himself to face up to and correct the problem of incompetent generalship in the West. Unless he did so the Rebels would (as they, in fact, did) eventually suffer total defeat—not just in the West but also everywhere else. As it was, any one of the western battles, campaigns, or operations (your choice) was the "decisive" military event that determined the outcome of the war.

That Elusive Turning Point

Many writers on the war, when not asserting, sometimes hysterically, that Gettysburg was the "decisive" battle of the conflict, occupy themselves proclaiming that engagement to have been the "turning point" of the war. On rare occasions some will label another struggle—Vicksburg, perhaps, or Shiloh, or even Atlanta—as the "turning point." Books and seminars on the conflict have been devoted to a consideration of "the turning *points*" (my emphasis) of the war. Perhaps the Civil War's military turning point is similar to those subatomic particles that, the people who study quantum mechanics tell us, can be in two places at once. (Could "quantum historians" locate it/them?)

As was the case with the term "decisive," the expression "turning point" can be used on any one of several different levels. A Confederate victory such as that in the Seven Days Battle of 1862 reversed a tide in Virginia that was clearly beginning to run in favor of the Federals. A battle could also turn nonmilitary aspects of the North-South struggle into a new channel—one leading to the Emancipation Proclamation, for example. Turning points can also be found within a battle. "Stonewall" Jackson's stand at First Manassas on July 21, 1861, and Sheridan's rallying the troops at the (actual) Battle of Cedar Creek stand as examples of this most limited of all kinds of military turning points. Finally, the words can be used in the highest sense to designate an event that diverted the overall military history of the war into a new channel. It is in this last sense that I apply the term here.

Viewing the war as a whole and considering the West as the area where the outcome of the conflict was determined, we can clearly see that the central military history of the war revolves around the story of Union armies marching from victory, to victory, to victory, to victory. This pattern held from the opening campaigns straight through to the final surrender of the Rebel armies. There was *never* a time when either the war in the West or the military events of the struggle taken as a whole were moving toward Confederate success or even hovering in neutral. There was, therefore, no overall military "turning point"—not at Gettysburg nor anywhere else.

To be sure, potential military turning points occurred in the West from time to time. The best came in the late summer and fall of 1862 when Rebel armies were advancing deep into Kentucky and back into northern Mississippi and northwestern Arkansas. A year later another potential turning point materialized in the aftermath of the secessionists' victory at Chickamauga. Had the western Rebel generals managed to convert either of those great opportunities into a strategic—or even a significant tactical—victory, they might well have altered the course of the war in some way. As it was, however, they failed to achieve any meaningful success at Perryville, Iuka, Corinth, Prairie Grove, or Chattanooga. Absent Southern success on the western battlefields, the war continued along in its old military course—stalemate in the East; victory for the Federal forces in the West and, ultimately, in the war.

If the war saw no military turning point, was there then some other type of change at a time when events that had been running in favor of the secessionists, or at least not against them, altered course in such a manner and to such a degree as to constitute a—or *the*—"turning point"? I believe so, and it is best called a geo-political-military turning point.

No state was more strategically located than was Kentucky, and no state proved more important in the eventual outcome of the war. If Kentucky joined the Confederacy, the broad Ohio River would become the northern political and military boundary of Rebeldom from the Appalachian Mountains to the Mississippi River. Faced with such an obstacle, the Federal government would find its military and political task exponentially more complex and difficult, especially given the strong pro-Confederate (or at least anti-Republican) sentiment that existed in much of southern Ohio, Indiana, and Illinois.

Should the Bluegrass State adhere to the Union, however, that northern military frontier of the Confederacy would shift more than two hundred miles southward to the Tennessee River—the next defensible line— and all of West and Middle Tennessee and part of northern Alabama would lie open to easy occupation by Federal troops. Without Kentucky, Confederate forces in the West would find themselves saddled with the probably impossible task of defending the open northern border of Tennessee, a line devoid of natural obstacles to an army's advance, penetrated by the Tennessee and Cumberland Rivers, and flanked on the west by the Mississippi River.

Governor Beriah Magoffin of Kentucky wished for his state to secede. The majority of the state legislature supported the Union. Most white Kentuckians seem simply to have hoped that the North-South conflict would go away and that some compromise could be found between the sections. White Kentuckians were proslavery and antisecession, and they did not want any part of the coming war.

Faced with such a divided citizenry, the state's politicians hit upon the bizarre policy of neutrality. Never mind that such a status would have been impossible to maintain. Kentucky simply could not have been a member of the Union and remain neutral in a war in which the United States was engaged and in which the state found herself on the boundary between the warring powers. (But how often have politicians made irrational, dishonest promises?) A modern analogy would be if Texas were to declare her neutrality in a war between the United States and

Mexico or Michigan were to do the same in a conflict between the United States and Canada.[18]

Jefferson Davis and Abraham Lincoln—both natives of the Bluegrass State—immediately realized the importance of Kentucky. "I would like to have God on my side," Lincoln is said once to have declared, "but I must have Kentucky." Not wanting to push the state into the arms of the other side, each chief executive quickly promised to respect Kentucky's neutral status, and each immediately set about surreptitiously subverting that neutrality and plotting to secure control of the Bluegrass for his cause.

In this delicate situation, Davis, therefore, did not dare have Confederate military forces operating openly in the state. The Rebel government, however, did send help to its supporters in Kentucky and set up recruiting stations and camps of instruction just south of the Kentucky-Tennessee border to give prosecessionists convenient places where they could come to join the Confederate army. All of those men who were of voting age, we should note, would have served the Confederacy far better had they remained at their homes to cast ballots for prosecession candidates in various political contests.

The Union government established its own camps along Kentucky's northern border and sent weapons and other aid to its supporters in the state. Eventually, Federal officials organized recruiting camps inside Kentucky, which after all was still a part of the Union.

Not long after July 13, 1861, when Leonidas Polk assumed command of the Rebel forces in West Tennessee, he began casting covetous eyes on the high bluffs that stretched along the left (east) bank of the Mississippi River at Columbus, Kentucky. From those heights, Polk reasoned, heavy Rebel guns could close the Great River to any Northern vessels that ventured downstream. Like most Confederates at the time, Polk assumed that a downriver thrust along the Mississippi would constitute

18. See Rossiter Johnson, "Turning-Points in the Civil War," *American Historical Association Annual Report for the Year 1894* (Washington: GPO, 1895), 39–53. James A. Rawley, in *Turning Points of the Civil War* (Lincoln: Univ. of Nebraska Press, 1966), presents a discussion of other crucial moments (not all of them military) when he thinks the war altered course. As this essay makes clear, I question Rawley's comments about several of the military events he cites.

the greatest threat to Tennessee, and he accordingly focused almost all of his attention and devoted most of his resources to defending that invasion route into the Central South.

Early in September 1861 Polk sent his troops marching across the state line to occupy Columbus. He acted in clear violation of his government's stated policy and without even informing the authorities in Richmond as to his intention. The horrified prosecession governor of Kentucky quickly appealed to those authorities to order Polk and his army out of the state. Jefferson Davis, doubtless misled by Polk's less-than-truthful justification for and explanation of his action, ignored the governor's demand as well as a similar one from the panicked chief executive of Tennessee, who saw his state now laid open to invasion all along her indefensible northern border. Davis even overruled his own secretary of war, Leroy Pope Walker, who had quickly telegraphed orders for Polk to withdraw to Tennessee, and allowed the general's violation of Kentucky's neutrality to stand.[19]

Although the Bluegrass State was clearly sliding away from the Confederacy by the late summer of 1861, and Federal forces almost certainly would have moved into Kentucky within a short time had Polk not acted when he did, every day—even every hour—that the state remained officially "neutral" and unoccupied by Federal troops redounded to the Confederacy's great advantage. Polk's violation of Kentucky's border was a major disaster for the Southern cause. The action branded the Rebels as aggressors and clearly demonstrated to all that the Confederacy had no regard for a state's right to decide her own destiny. It convinced a clear majority of Kentuckians to support the Union, and ultimately the state furnished as many soldiers to the Federal cause as did Massachusetts. The end of Kentucky's neutrality laid the entire northern boundary of Tennessee open to invasion. Worst of all for the secessionists' immediate interests, Polk's shortsighted action secured no significant military advantage for the Confederacy.

19. See Steven E. Woodworth, "'The Indeterminate Quantities': Jefferson Davis, Leonidas Polk, and the End of Kentucky Neutrality," *Civil War History* 38 (1992): 289–97.

As soon as Brig. Gen. Ulysses S. Grant, at his base in Cairo, Illinois, learned of Polk's rash act, he dispatched some of his troops up the Ohio River to seize Paducah, Kentucky, at the mouth of the Tennessee River and Smithland, Kentucky, at the mouth of the Cumberland. With Paducah in their hands the Yankees could easily move south up the Tennessee River and outflank Columbus to the west. Polk and his force would then have to choose between abandoning their fortified position on the Mississippi or being cut off and trapped there. When Grant did advance up the Tennessee a few months later, the Rebels evacuated Columbus without firing a shot.

Polk's violation of Kentucky's neutral status became the key that opened up the West to Union naval and military power. A neutral Kentucky protected the northern border of Tennessee and the Confederacy from Yankee forces and closed the Tennessee and Cumberland Rivers to Federal gunboats far more effectively than Confederate fortifications and armies ever could have. After early September 1861 the Rebels' best (indeed, their only) natural military line of defense in the West was the Tennessee River. One of the greatest problems facing secessionist military commanders in the region after Polk's incursion into Kentucky was the fact that politics, economics, logistics, diplomacy, and public opinion all compelled them to try to hold the area north of the Tennessee River, while military logic dictated that they should abandon the region or at least not commit great resources to an effort to maintain possession of it.[20]

All of the early 1862 disasters that the Confederates suffered at Mill Springs, Fort Henry, Fort Donelson, Shiloh, and Island Number Ten stemmed directly from Polk's actions during September 1861. So too (at least in part) did the defeats of 1862 and 1863 in central and southeastern

20. J. F. C. Fuller argued that "the strategic frontier" of the Confederacy in the West ran along the Tennessee River and that, therefore, the secessionists should have held that line in force and kept only small outposts in Tennessee and Kentucky. *Grant and Lee: A Study in Personality and Generalship* (Bloomington: Indiana Univ. Press, 1957), 32–33. In purely (and shortsighted) military terms, Fuller's idea makes sense, but from all other perspectives it would have been extremely foolish for the Rebel government willingly to have abandoned almost an entire state—especially one as important as Tennessee.

Tennessee. Even some of the great losses that the Southerners experienced in the Mississippi Valley in 1863 (Arkansas Post and Vicksburg) grew indirectly out of Polk's 1861 invasion of Kentucky. Those losses, of course, might—indeed probably would—eventually have taken place anyway. As it was, however, they resulted from Polk's gross misconduct. Had those defeats been postponed, say, three to twelve months, the Rebels' chances of winning their independence by not losing the war would have been greatly enhanced.

Until early September 1861 the Confederacy had experienced no serious reverse of any kind anywhere. The Rebels had declared their independence, organized their national government, raised a large and powerful army, and won three significant battles (First Manassas in Virginia and Wilson's Creek and Lexington in Missouri). Events up to that time were running in the secessionists' favor—or, at least, not moving against them. Polk's strike into Kentucky and Grant's response in seizing Paducah and Smithland reversed that situation. From September 1861, overall Confederate military fortunes ran in an unbending and unbroken line straight downhill. The Rebels could never find a general in the West who could reverse or even significantly retard the tide that turned and began to flow against them when Polk's men marched into Kentucky. Eventually that tide would carry them on to final and total defeat.

The Western Paradigm and the Union

Most of the earlier sections of this part have dealt with the Confederate war effort or with factors that affected both North and South rather than with those pertaining only to the Federal side of the struggle. This imbalance has been owing largely to the fact that, over the decades, discussion of the outcome of the war has more often focused on the Confederates and the reason or reasons for their defeat rather than on the unionists and the reason or reasons for their victory. Historians have usually not applied Maj. Gen. George E. Pickett's explanation for the outcome of the Battle of Gettysburg—"I always thought that the Yankees had something to do with it"—to the outcome of the war.

Students of the North-South conflict, it seems, have chosen to devote more of their time and attention to the Rebels than they have to the Northerners. The natural consequence has been that the literature dealing with the Confederate side of the war is considerably more voluminous than is that devoted to the Federal war effort. When we turn to the Union side of the struggle, however, we find that once again the western paradigm can help us gain a better understanding of the war's overall military history.

Application of the new way of viewing the struggle to the Federal side of Civil War military history sheds much light on the problems with which the national government had to deal (many of them, as we shall see, of its own making) and why the Union armies eventually triumphed despite those difficulties.

The basic reason why the Federals ultimately prevailed is very simple: The fundamental grand strategy that produced final victory for the U.S. government very closely approximated the fundamental approach to the war that a Union general who understood and embraced the western paradigm would have adopted. This development, in turn, took the Northern armies into a region (the West) where geography and the poor quality of the opposing generals combined with lesser factors to bring victory after victory to the Yankees.

To a very slight extent this (for the unionists, fortuitous) development resulted from planning. Sheer, blind luck was a greater factor. Mostly, however, it grew from one key circumstance—the inability of the Federal armies to achieve success in Virginia. In fact, the Northern forces were compelled to follow a western paradigm grand strategy by the Confederates—or, to be more accurate, by Gen. Robert E. Lee. (See Part 6.)

The complete story, however, is more complex. Although several important Yankees grasped the crucial significance of the West (Ulysses Grant, William T. Sherman, Henry Halleck, and Governor Oliver P. Morton of Indiana, among others), the Federal authorities in Washington never overtly adopted a grand strategy based on the western paradigm. In fact, for virtually the entire war, they sought to achieve military victory through some other plan. Accordingly, they devoted a great deal of effort and committed considerable resources to what were, in truth, literally peripheral operations.

In so doing, they recklessly spent the lives of thousands of good soldiers, diverted the greater part of the public's attention from the key military operations, gave the Confederates hope and a reason to continue the fight, and on occasion brought the Union cause close to failure. They also created the intellectual framework that has diverted large numbers of historians as well as the general public from the war's most important military operations for well over a century.

In the spring of 1861, at the very beginning of the conflict, the aged Winfield Scott, commanding general of the U.S. Army, recommended an overall war plan to Federal authorities. Scott proposed that the unionists establish a naval blockade along the Atlantic and Gulf coasts to isolate the seceded states from outside help. While the Northerners waited for the blockade to take effect, the Federal government would raise, equip, and train a large and powerful army.

Once that army was ready and cooler fall weather had reduced the chances of disease in the Deep South, Scott proposed, the national government should send a strong force down the Mississippi River to slice the Confederacy in half. Sealed off from all outside help, their would-be nation cut in twain, and their largest, most important city and chief port (New Orleans) occupied by hostile forces, the secessionists would soon lose political control to local pro-Union men. Once in power, these loyalists would quickly return their states to their old places in the Union. The war would thus end with a national victory, minimum loss of life, and but slight disruption of American society.

Political authorities rejected Scott's plan because they believed that even if it worked, it would require too large an army, cost too much, and take too long for an impatient public. Some members of the press derided it as "the anaconda plan" (so called because its objective was to squeeze the Confederacy to death as a constrictor crushes its prey). The old general soon found himself shunted off into retirement.

In truth, however, Scott's concept was a well-thought-out blueprint that foreshadowed the grand strategy Union forces would follow to eventual victory. The great campaigns that brought ultimate success to the Federal cause were either operations that were a direct part of the plan Scott had recommended (Fort Henry, Fort Donelson, Shiloh, Island Number Ten, New Orleans, Arkansas Post, Vicksburg, Port Hudson) or the natural evolutionary outgrowth of Scott's grand strategy (most of the major 1863–65 operations in Tennessee, Georgia, and the Carolinas).

As the Federal government followed Scott's recommendations over the next four years, it met with success; when it deviated from the counsel of the wise old general, it usually met with failure and on several occasions brought itself close to disaster. Even when successful in such deviations, Northern forces accomplished nothing of great or lasting importance and sometimes paid an unusually high price in casualties. Persistence in such efforts by Union authorities, however, offered the Confederates their best chance to gain national independence.

At the very opening of the conflict, Federal leaders made a major deviation from Scott's recommendation. Virginia was the second largest (after Texas), most populous, economically most developed, and—with her history and long list of distinguished men—most prestigious of the Confederate states. Soon after her secession, the Rebels shifted their capital from Montgomery, Alabama, to Richmond, thereby making the Old Dominion the political heart of the Confederacy. Virginia's capital thus became, in the word of historian Archer Jones, a "magnet," her allure drawing public and governmental attention from both the North and the South.[21]

Lusting after Richmond, Northern authorities decided to begin (and eventually to continue all through the war) large-scale operations in Virginia aimed at the capture of the secessionists' capital and/or the destruction of the Southern army defending it. In so doing, they made the classic mistake of attacking their enemy at his strongest, most visible point rather than where he was most vulnerable.

21. Jones, *Civil War Command and Strategy: The Process of Victory and Defeat* (New York: Free Press, 1992), 40. See also the arguments in Weigley, *Great Civil War,* summarized above in note 5.

Once embarked on this costly and misguided grand strategy, the Federal political leaders found themselves trapped. As the Yankees launched one highly publicized "On to Richmond" drive after another, public opinion and the press came to focus even more attention on military events in the East, almost to the exclusion of what was happening elsewhere. Virginia, after all, was very close to the North's great centers of population, commerce, and journalism, and most of the Union troops who served in the Old Dominion were from the populous, nearby states of the Northeast. It was natural, therefore, that they and their families and friends at home as well as the press concentrate on the campaigns in the East.

Given this situation, Union authorities continued throughout the conflict to commit large numbers of troops and virtually all of the national prestige to the struggle in Virginia. Many of them, furthermore, honestly if erroneously, believed that the road to Richmond was the only route to victory and that the only road to Richmond ran southward from Washington on the Potomac to the Rebel capital on the James.

At the beginning of the war this strategy could be justified. A smashing Union victory in Virginia would almost certainly have brought about a quick end to the rebellion. As the conflict wore on, however, the fallacy in this course of action became increasingly obvious, but the authorities never abandoned it. In effect, they confused defeating the Confederates in Virginia with defeating the Confederacy. Tens of thousands of Americans paid for this misjudgment with their lives, and scores of thousands of others with painful, often crippling wounds.

Early in 1864 the U.S. Congress passed a bill reviving the grade of lieutenant general (held earlier only by George Washington, although the aged Winfield Scott then held it by brevet). The revived grade was intended for Ulysses Grant, whose 1862–63 victories at Fort Donelson, Shiloh, Vicksburg, and Chattanooga had demonstrated his great ability as a commander and as an organizer of victory. With his new lieutenant general's commission, Grant would outrank all other Union officers. (As a major general, Grant stood subordinate to several senior major generals, some of them of at best mediocre ability.) Early in March 1864 Lincoln summoned Grant to Washington, and in a White House ceremony he formally presented the general with his new commission and named him commander of all Union land forces.

With Grant's appointment, the Federal armies had for the first time an overall commander with the legal authority to direct their operations, the ability to devise sound plans, the willpower to see that the armies followed his plans, and the full support of the government. Then, having taken the wise step of unifying the national forces under Grant's command, President Lincoln and the Northern authorities made a great personnel blunder—their worst of the war.

In March 1864, when Grant came to Washington to receive his new commission and assignment, he intended to return to the West, where he had won such great victories in 1862 and 1863 and where he planned to direct the 1864 operations in person. Most of the Yankees' western armies were then wintering in southeastern Tennessee near Chattanooga, resting and preparing for the next campaign. They were poised to sweep into Georgia and Alabama when spring came in 1864. Then, Grant hoped, he would advance the area under Union control from the Tennessee River southward along a line running from Chattanooga to Atlanta, Georgia, and thence southwest into Alabama through Montgomery and on to Mobile on the Gulf of Mexico. Success in such a campaign would bisect the Confederacy east of the Mississippi River as Grant's earlier operations in the Valley of the Mississippi had cut the Rebel nation in half along that waterway.

Unfortunately for the Union cause and for tens of thousands of Civil War soldiers both North and South, Grant soon changed his mind—or maybe political authorities in Washington changed it for him. Grant (or Lincoln) decided that the new lieutenant general should transfer to the eastern theater and assume personal direction of the major Federal army there during its 1864 campaign against Lee. This decision brought Grant, by far the best of the Federal generals, to the Old Dominion and pitted him against Lee, the Confederacy's only competent army commander. It also meant that the Yankees would attempt to make their main 1864 effort in Virginia.

These changes confined Grant to the one area where the Rebels were at their strongest, where local geography and the Confederate infra-structure most helped them, and where the best Confederate army and the South's one capable army commander were able to nullify Grant's great ability.

The result of the decision to shift Grant to Virginia and launch the main 1864 Union effort there was a series of great, bloody, indecisive battles in the Old Dominion. The only military results of those engagements were horrific casualty lists, preservation of the stalemate that had existed in the East since the summer of 1861, and—most important—the ab-sence of Grant from western operations. Those casualties and that stale-mate, in turn, cast a deep gloom over the people of the Northern states that summer and convinced many of them—including, at times, Lincoln himself—that the president would be defeated in the fall election.[22]

22. I believe that meaningful consideration of the grand strategy of the war—at least so far as a possible favorable outcome for the Confederacy is concerned—has to be cut off with the (actual) 1864 election. Given Lincoln's commitment to preserving the Union, nothing short of divine intervention could have saved the Confederacy after the president's November 1864 victory at the polls. There can be no doubt that once Lincoln had secured a second term, the Federal government would see the war through to final, complete victory.

Several friends who have critiqued this essay or with whom I have discussed the matter raised the point that public opinion in the North demanded that the national government prosecute the war in Virginia and, in effect, compelled Lincoln to bring Grant to the East to face Lee. Beyond question the public focused on the operations in Virginia. We can, however, wonder to what degree military strategy should be dictated by public opinion. Would not public opinion in the aftermath of Pearl Harbor have dictated that the major American effort in World War II be di-rected against Japan rather than against Germany, the more dangerous enemy? We should also remember that in the Civil War, the public could not express its opinion until November 1864.

I suspect that if Grant had compelled the Confederacy to surrender in, say, July or August 1864 by winning a great victory in Georgia and destroying the Rebel army there or had he marched his forces into Richmond from the south rather than across the bloody battlefields of the Old Dominion, most Northerners would happily have accepted victory rather than de-manding that he then fight it out with Lee.

Other critics have suggested that Grant made Sherman's success possible by penning Lee down in Virginia and thus preventing him from detaching troops to reinforce other Rebel armies or by preventing Lee from moving across the Potomac as he had done in 1862 and 1863. If, however, the purpose of the Union's 1864 operations in Virginia was to hold Lee in position by hurling one massive attack after another against his impregnable fortifications, then surely some general other than Grant could have directed those efforts. Ambrose Burnside, for one, had demonstrated at Fredericksburg in December 1862 that he was quite skilled in conducting

Grant then compounded this first error with what I believe to have been a second major miscalculation. As his replacement to command the western Union armies, he selected Maj. Gen. William T. Sherman. Sherman was Grant's trusted friend, his lieutenant in many of the great western triumphs, a very intelligent man, and a general who had (or would soon develop) a grasp of warfare on a geopolitical-psychological level that put him far in advance of almost all of his contemporaries.

Sherman was not, however, a skilled battlefield commander, and he almost totally lacked the killer instinct to destroy the enemy army in his front. Twice in 1864 he was to be presented with perfect opportunities when in all probability he could have delivered a knockout blow to the Confederate army that opposed him in North Georgia and hence to the secessionist cause. The first came early in May at Snake Creek Gap, when he could easily have put an overwhelming force across his opponent's line of supply, cut off the Rebels from their base, and trapped them in the North Georgia mountains. The second occurred in early September, when he stood with six powerful infantry corps in the midst of a confused, defeated, demoralized Confederate army that was then separated into three weak, isolated segments. In both cases Sherman, who had little taste for battle, *chose* to allow the enemy force to march away to fight again another day. This, we should note, was the exact opposite of the way Grant wanted the 1864 campaigns conducted.

It is inconceivable that Grant or Maj. Gen. George H. Thomas, the logical alternative to Sherman as commander in the West, would have

---

such operations. Thus, the North's best general could have been better employed in more important campaigns elsewhere. With regard to the second point, it seems obvious that if Lee could not win the war against McClellan, Pope, Burnside, and Hooker, he would not have won it against Meade.

Even if the Federals still had to overcome Lee's army after concluding successful campaigns in the West, they would have been far more likely to have succeeded with their western armies united with the Yankees in Virginia for the final operations.

Finally, we should note that Grant's 1864 Overland campaign failed even to keep Lee from detaching troops to operate elsewhere. He did, after all, send Jubal Early off to the Shenandoah Valley with about one-fourth of the Army of Northern Virginia. On this point, see McMurry, *Atlanta,* app. 1, 191–93.

allowed the secessionist army to escape on either of those occasions without at least making an effort to destroy it. On both occasions, in fact, Thomas urged Sherman to try to finish off the Rebels. Success in such an effort would have shortened the war by many months and saved the thousands of lives that were expended in later battles made necessary by Sherman's failure—indeed, his refusal—to exploit the opportunities that came his way in May and/or September 1864.[23]

Had the Federal authorities allowed Grant to remain in the West for the 1864 campaign—as Grant had originally intended to do and as Sherman himself urged—and had they not persisted in throwing men into the Virginia meatgrinder (to borrow a term from a later and even greater war), victory for the national forces would almost certainly have come much sooner and at far less human and financial cost. The Yankees in the East—as they demonstrated in 1862 and 1863—were quite capable of preventing the Rebels from winning the war in that theater (if not always capable of preventing them from winning battles there). The western Confederate generals, as they demonstrated repeatedly throughout the war, were incapable of stopping the Federal juggernaut that, in all probability, needed only Grant's (or Thomas's) sure hand to drive through to what would have been a final triumph in the late spring or summer of 1864. Such a victory would have dissolved all doubt about both the ultimate outcome of the war and the reelection of Abraham Lincoln long before voters in the North went to the polls that fall. Sherman, of course, eventually won for the Union in Georgia in 1864, but I believe either Grant or Thomas would have secured the victory there sooner and at far less overall cost to the nation.

As mentioned above, the unionists confused defeating Lee in Virginia with defeating the Confederacy. The price for this mistake was paid

---

23. Thomas outranked Sherman and had enjoyed a more distinguished career, but Grant did not trust him to exercise overall command in the West. For that reason, perhaps, the selection of Sherman as Grant's successor in the overall western command was justified. For details of my thinking on these matters and comments about several other occasions when Sherman probably could have dealt the Rebels a severe, if not fatal, blow in Georgia that summer, see McMurry, *Atlanta*.

by the common soldiers in blood, pain, and suffering and by their families, who lost husbands, sons, brothers, and fathers in great but unnecessary battles that produced no significant results. The Northerners were fortunate in being able to mount more than one major military operation at a time and in being able to afford major mistakes—luxuries that the Confederacy did not have (this, by the way, is how the North's overwhelming strength ultimately paid off for the Federals). Eventual national victory has concealed the great fallacy in the Union's grand strategy for 1864.[24]

An old military saw has it that two things are necessary for an army to gain a great battlefield victory: a very good general on one side and a very bad general on the other. In 1862 and 1863 this condition worked in favor of the Yankees in the West, and Grant won the striking victories he achieved over Floyd, Pillow, Pemberton, and Bragg. By moving Grant to Virginia in 1864 and replacing him in the West with Sherman,

---

24. J. F. C. Fuller points out the mistake that Federal authorities made by stressing the war in Virginia rather than by concentrating against the Rebels' weak point in the West ("weakness accentuated undermines strength"). *Lee and Grant,* 41–42. He then failed to draw the obvious conclusions from this strategic insight and argued that Grant's purpose in 1864 was to hold Lee in position while Sherman outflanked him through Georgia and the Carolinas. As mentioned above, had that been the Union purpose, it could have been accomplished at far less human cost and by almost any Federal general.

I do think that had the war not ended as it did, Grant would have eventually worn down Lee's army by sheer attrition and thereby secured victory. Such a success, however, would have come sometime later (possibly not in time to save Lincoln in the election or before Sherman's force arrived in Virginia after his march through Georgia and the Carolinas). If this speculation is correct and we discount Grant's sometimes brilliant tactical moves in the 1864 campaign, we must ask if we are then back at the old and now usually discarded view of "Grant the butcher" rather than the current understanding that he was a skillful commander. Russell Weigley comes very close to taking this position, arguing that in 1864 Grant set out to defeat Lee by maneuver as he had done against Pemberton in Mississippi in 1863. His effort against Lee failed completely, and, Weigley states, Grant then resorted to a war of attrition ("Grant's familiar strategy of annihilation") in an effort to destroy Lee's army. "By midsummer [1864]," writes Weigley, "Grant had almost expended an entire army and had to replace it with another, but this outpouring of casualties was his only means of imposing enough casualties upon the enemy to win the complete and final victory." *Great Civil War,* 336, 347, 357, 371. What, we may ask, was going on in the West?

Federal authorities brought to an end the great command advantage that their forces had earlier enjoyed in the West without securing any compensating gain in the East. The result was the long, hot, bloody summer of 1864 during which final victory for the Union hovered in the balance for months longer than otherwise would have been the case.

PART SIX

Robert E. Lee and the Confederacy's Conduct of the War

Over the last three or four decades, what was once virtually un-thinkable in Civil War circles has become fairly common. Writers who dare to take a critical attitude toward Gen. Robert E. Lee have come out of the closet and created what amounts to a cottage industry dedicated to the production of books and articles in which they take the great Confederate commander to task for one or more of a large number of alleged weaknesses, flaws, faults, and character, psychological, or personality disorders. These assorted liabilities, they assert, explain not only the defeat of Lee's army in Virginia but also the ultimate failure of the Confederacy's bid for independence. Only recently have Lee's advocates rallied to mount an effective countereffort in the general's behalf.

For more than half a century after his death in October 1870, Robert E. Lee, in the words of writer Lamont Buchanan, "rode serenely along" high above the storm of historical debate that swirled constantly about almost all the other major figures of the 1861–65 period. Lee, Buchanan noted, had been "respected even by those who opposed the cause he served."[1]

Lee acquired, first, the status of a (really *the*) great hero of the white South, and then after several decades he became also a major national figure, admired and respected by almost all white Americans, North and South, for his high personal character, flawless life, and unquestioned personal integrity. During those decades almost all commentators on the Civil War also pronounced him the conflict's greatest military genius and one of the few truly great military commanders in the nation's, if not the world's, history.

1. Buchanan, *A Pictorial History of the Confederacy* (New York: Crown, 1951), 98.

This view of Lee was in large part reality. After all, he was a very good general as well as a man of extraordinary personal integrity, intelligence, and ability. In part too this view stemmed from the ceaseless post-1870 activities of such often overlapping groups as the Lee Memorial Association, "Early and company," the Southern Historical Society, the United Confederate Veterans, the Confederated Southern Memorial Association, the United Daughters of the Confederacy, and the Sons of Confederate Veterans.

The Lee depicted by these organizations quickly made his way into the history books thanks to the prominent historians of the late nineteenth and early twentieth centuries. He thereby became a fixture of popular culture and of textbooks and courses in American history at all levels and in schools all across the country, if not the English-speaking world.

This—what we may call the traditional—picture of Lee as a military genius and a near-saint reached its apogee, so far at least, in Douglas Southall Freeman's mid-1930s Pulitzer Prize–winning, four-volume *R. E. Lee*. Several subsequent writers, notably Clifford Dowdey, have echoed this almost hagiographic general view of Lee to a greater or lesser extent. In the popular mind Lee still enjoys this status.[2]

While the great majority of the war's participants and students spent their time extolling Lee as a great, if not the conflict's greatest, military commander, a few did venture on occasion to criticize his generalship—although usually in more-or-less muted, inconspicuous ways. Even during the war an informal "western concentration bloc" consisting of several high-ranking Confederate military and political figures mounted a challenge to Lee's views on the conflict and his conduct of military operations. Gen. Pierre G. T. Beauregard was the most prominent spokesman for this informal group and the officer who most frequently expressed doubts about Lee's views on grand strategy.

2. Dowdey, *Lee* (Boston: Little Brown, 1965). For a more balanced view that incorporates most of the recent work on Lee, see Emory M. Thomas, *Robert E. Lee: A Biography* (New York: W. W. Norton, 1995).

While they often disagreed among themselves about various matters, members of the western concentration bloc were united by the belief that the Confederate government habitually allocated too many men and too much of the Rebels' limited military resources to Lee's war effort in Virginia. Instead, Beauregard and his colleagues argued, the Southerners should stand on the defensive in the East and commit more of their troops and resources to the secessionist armies in Tennessee and/or Mississippi—even if they had to take those troops and resources from Lee's force in Virginia to do so. Members of the bloc expressed, usually in carping letters to each other, serious reservations about Lee's aggressive style of warfare in the East, especially the two great offensive campaigns that he waged beyond the Potomac (Antietam in 1862 and Gettysburg in 1863). They tried, without much success, to steer Rebel military policy into channels other than those advocated by Lee.

The fact that many leading members of the bloc were bitter personal, political, and/or professional enemies of President Jefferson Davis and members of his cabinet proved a great handicap to their cause. The additional facts that the generals in the bloc usually mismanaged their own military operations and at times refused to cooperate or even communicate with the government also weakened both their arguments and their influence with Richmond authorities. For these reasons and also because of his own personality, his respectful attitude toward and willingness to cooperate with the government and keep Confederate officials informed, and—above all—his battlefield successes, Lee had more influence with the Davis administration and usually carried the day in the debates over grand strategy, although the government did not always adopt his ideas in toto.[3]

During the postwar years James Longstreet ventured to voice publicly his doubts about some of Lee's military decisions, especially Lee's aggressive conduct of the Battle of Gettysburg. Longstreet's criticisms of his old commander added fuel to the attacks that Early and company

---

3. Thomas Lawrence Connelly and Archer Jones, *The Politics of Command: Factions and Ideas in Confederate Strategy* (Baton Rouge: Louisiana State Univ. Press, 1973), especially chap. 3.

launched against him. Former brigadier general E. Porter Alexander, who during the war had been one of the more capable young officers in the Army of Northern Virginia, also expressed similar criticism of Lee's decisions at Gettysburg in his *Military Memoirs of a Confederate* (published in 1907) as well as in some of his other writings. Both Longstreet and Alexander were especially critical of Lee's tactical aggressiveness at Gettysburg—his determination to attack and then to renew the attack on the very strong Federal position along the ridges and hills south of the town.

On occasion a few Northern veterans also voiced doubts about Lee's performance as an army commander. In 1878 Lt. Gen. (and then former president) Ulysses S. Grant, Lee's last opponent, told a newspaper reporter that he had never shared the very high opinion of Lee then held by so many others. Grant, in fact, claimed to have worried more when he faced Confederate troops commanded by Gen. Joseph E. Johnston than he had when Lee stood in his front. Lee, Grant opined, had been "a fair commander" of a "slow, conservative, cautious nature."[4]

In 1913 George A. Bruce, who had served as a staff officer in the Union army during the war, published a long article in which he expressed doubts about many facets of Lee's conduct of military operations while in command of the Army of Northern Virginia. Bruce's highly critical remarks adumbrated almost all of the unfavorable comments about Lee's generalship, battles, and campaigns that later writers were to develop in much more detail.[5]

4. See Gary W. Gallagher, ed., *Lee: The Soldier* (Lincoln: Univ. of Nebraska Press, 1996), xxi–xxii. Grant, we should note, never really commanded troops who operated against Johnston (who in any case enjoyed a vastly inflated reputation that he could never do anything to justify). The only times Grant and Johnston faced each other came during the Vicksburg campaign (May–July 1863), when Johnston with a tiny, ineffective force hovered in west-central Mississippi trying without success to find some way to pry Grant out of his massive fortifications around Vicksburg and thereby save the garrison of that doomed city, and in the Chattanooga–North Georgia area during the winter of 1863–64 (December–March) while the two were trying to prepare their respective armies for the next campaign. If Grant did make and mean such a statement, that fact alone is sufficient to take his own reputation as a commander down a dozen or so notches.

5. Bruce, "The Strategy of the Civil War," *Military Historical Society of Massachusetts Papers,* 13 (1913), 393–483 (especially 444–83). The relevant parts of Bruce's article as well as many of the other writings on Lee can be found in Gallagher, *Lee.*

Low-key criticism of Lee continued in the decades after World War I. Even as Douglas Southall Freeman labored over his great biography of Lee, J. F. C. Fuller, a British general, embarked on the task of boosting Ulysses S. Grant's reputation. Concluding that Grant had been the greatest commander of the war, Fuller often digressed from his immediate subject to comment unfavorably on what he regarded as Lee's generally poor performance while in command of the Army of Northern Virginia.[6]

In more recent decades Thomas Lawrence Connelly and Alan T. Nolan have taken up the task of critically evaluating Lee and his Civil War record. In addition to accepting and expanding much of the work of earlier writers, especially that of Bruce and Fuller, Connelly and Nolan broadened their inquiries to include comments on Lee's personality, his marriage, and his ideas about several nonmilitary subjects as well as his general conduct of army operations and his views on grand strategy.

Connelly took Lee to task for his alleged overemphasis on the war in Virginia to the neglect of the strategically more important western Confederacy. He also raised a number of questions about Lee the human, as differentiated from Lee the general, branding him an insecure man, "an unfulfilled person" trapped in an unsatisfactory marriage, a man who held "a low opinion of himself," a complex man characterized by "savage outbursts of temper . . . , deep moods of depression . . . , [a] long-time fixation with death . . . , [and] troubled . . . [by] elements of frustration, self doubt, and unhappiness." Connelly's troubled, unhappy Lee was quite different from Freeman's simple, saintly, knightly, Christian gentleman. In effect, Connelly argued that Lee was a human being with emotions, problems, and a temper that he usually kept under control only by great efforts.

The high esteem in which Lee had so long been held was, Connelly asserted (in the face—it must be said—of overwhelming evidence to the contrary), mostly the product of postwar writings by white Southerners seeking to assuage the pain of their defeat and to sanctify the Lost Cause of the 1860s. To do so they created the myth of Lee as a near-perfect man

6. Fuller, *Grant and Lee;* and *The Generalship of Ulysses S. Grant* (London: Eyre and Spottiswiide, 1929).

and a flawless soldier and portrayed him as the embodiment of the white South in general and of the Confederate South in particular.

Maintaining that Lee had never received adequate consideration from brainwashed historians and biographers, Alan T. Nolan undertook a thorough, lawyerlike examination of what he called "the Lee dogma" and sought to delineate "the historic as opposed to the mythic Lee." This quest led Nolan into an examination of Lee's ideas on secession, slavery and race relations, government, Reconstruction, and several of the other issues that had loomed so large in mid-nineteenth-century America. By showing that Lee had shared the beliefs on such subjects held by most others of his race, his time, his region, and his class, Nolan in effect demonstrated that Lee had been a white, mid-nineteenth-century, Southern aristocrat. Nolan also devoted a long chapter of his book to a critique of Lee's role in Confederate military history. Michael Fellman has recently produced a politically correct book-length treatment of the Connelly-Nolan Lee, adding a critique of the general's racism, sexism, and Southern nationalism as well as an attack on the traditional view of "Saint Robert" and the code of the white South. Fellman, however, shuns almost entirely any serious discussion of Lee as a Confederate general and his military strategy.[7]

Meanwhile, a pack of other writers has taken out after Lee, its members stressing almost exclusively what they regard as his deficiencies as an army commander and/or as a maker of Confederate grand strategy. Bevin Alexander, Edward H. Bonekemper III, John D. McKenzie, and Michael A. Palmer constitute the best-known members of this group. Almost all of their ideas are simply variations on or elaborations of one or more of the contentions put forth by earlier critics, especially those of Bruce, Fuller, and Nolan.[8] Only the subject of Lee as a Rebel general concerns us here.

7. Connelly, "Robert E. Lee and the Western Confederacy: A Criticism of Lee's Strategic Ability," *Civil War History* 15 (1969): 116–32; and *The Marble Man: Robert E. Lee and His Image in American History* (New York: Alfred E. Knopf, 1977); Nolan, *Lee Considered: General Robert E. Lee and Civil War History* (Chapel Hill: Univ. of North Carolina Press, 1991); Fellman, *The Making of Robert E. Lee* (New York: Random House, 2000).

8. Alexander, *Lost Victories: The Military Genius of Stonewall Jackson* (New York: Henry Holt, 1992)—in which he argues that Jackson, not Lee, was the Rebel commander who best under-

CONDUCT OF THE WAR

Even as Lee has come under increasing criticism as a military commander, he has gained the support of a group of modern historians who have galloped to his defense. While not subscribing to the old view of Lee the perfect man and the infallible general, Albert Castel, Charles P. Roland, Gary W. Gallagher, Joseph Glatthaar, and Joseph Harsh constitute a most able quintet of scholars who take a basically favorable overall view of Lee as a Confederate commander. In my opinion they have pretty much demolished the criticisms that Lee's detractors have made about the general's military role in the war, although they willingly admit that he did make mistakes—especially in ordering the massive assaults on the very strong Union positions at Malvern Hill and Gettysburg. As a group, however, these defenders have often overlooked a major factor in their critique of both Lee and his critics.[9]

Over the years Lee's critics have raised several questions about such facets of the general's command as his inadequate, overworked staff; his alleged failure to discipline unruly subordinates or to dispose of incompetent ones (he has also been faulted for dumping incompetent subordinates onto other Rebel armies); his vague orders and practice of allowing subordinates too much discretion; his poor handling of logistics; his foolish

---

stood the nature of the struggle and proposed a realistic strategy to win Southern independence, while "Lee's course guaranteed a Union triumph" (xii)—and *Robert E. Lee's Civil War* (Holbrook, Mass.: Adams Media, 1998); Bonekemper, *How Robert E. Lee Lost the Civil War* (Fredericksburg, Va.: Sergeant Kirkland's Press, 1997); McKenzie, *Uncertain Glory: Lee's Generalship Re-Examined* (New York: Hippocrene, 1997); Palmer, *Lee Moves North: Robert E. Lee on the Offensive from Antietam to Gettysburg* (New York: John Wiley & Sons, 1998).

9. Castel, "The Historian and the General: Thomas Lawrence Connelly versus Robert E. Lee," *Civil War History* 16 (1970), 50–63; Roland, *Reflections on Lee: A Historian's Assessment* (Mechanicsburg, Pa.: Stackpole, 1995); Gallagher, *The Confederate War: How Popular Will, Nationalism, and Military Strategy Could Not Stave Off Defeat* (Cambridge, Mass.: Harvard Univ. Press, 1997); Glatthaar, *Partners in Command: The Relationships between Leaders in the Civil War* (New York: Free Press, 1994); Harsh, *Confederate Tide Rising: Robert E. Lee and the Making of Southern Strategy, 1861–1862,* and *Taken at the Flood: Robert E. Lee and Confederate Strategy in the Maryland Campaign of 1862* (Kent, Ohio: Kent State Univ. Press, 1998, 1999). The special "Robert E. Lee Issue" of *North & South* (3.5 [June 2000]) contains several articles by both Lee's critics and his defenders. John M. Taylor's *Duty Faithfully Performed: Robert E. Lee and His Critics* (Dulles, Va.: Brassey's, 1999) is a much weaker defense of Lee but does contain some valuable insights; see especially 228–39.

reliance on easily misunderstood verbal rather than written orders; and his conduct of this or that battle and/or campaign.

The major issues in the criticism of Lee's Confederate military role boil down to three crucial points: that Lee was an old-fashioned—even medieval—military figure more suited to the warfare of the seventeenth (or even of the twelfth) century than to a modern nineteenth-century industrial war; that he was obsessed with the defense of Virginia and had very little interest in and almost no knowledge of the Confederacy beyond the boundaries of the Old Dominion; and that Lee's propensity to pursue a "decisive" battlefield victory led him to wage a foolish, counterproductive, and unnecessary offensive war at both the tactical and strategic levels and, in so doing, to squander the South's most valuable military resource—her manpower.

Gary W. Gallagher has recently dealt with the allegation that Lee was an old-fashioned commander hopelessly unsuited to direct the operations of a mid-nineteenth-century army. I have nothing to add to his conclusion that the general "was an able practitioner of modern mid-nineteenth century warfare." The remainder of this part of the essay will be devoted to the two other major issues.[10]

Lee's critics maintain that the general's commitment to the secessionist cause did not extend much beyond his determination to protect his native Virginia from Yankee invasion and that he consistently subordinated larger considerations of Confederate national interests to that goal. The allegation is nothing new. "His Virginia was his world," commented William T. Sherman in 1887.[11]

The critics assert that Lee's alleged parochialism combined with his ignorance of conditions in the West in such a way that he misunderstood completely the situation beyond the Alleghenies and therefore entertained very unrealistic notions about both the area and the problems that Confed-

10. Gallagher, "An Old-Fashioned Soldier in a Modern War: Robert E. Lee as a Confederate General," *Civil War History* 45 (1999): 295–321.

11. Quoted in Michael Fellman, *Citizen Sherman: A Life of William Tecumseh Sherman* (New York: Random House, 1995), 406.

erate armies faced there. The critics maintain that Lee's proximity to Richmond and his great influence with President Davis, along with his general ignorance of western matters and his bias toward Virginia, led to a misallocation of Rebel resources and a concentration of secessionist strength in the Old Dominion. The end result, they believe, was a fatally flawed grand strategy that produced eventual total defeat for the Confederacy.

Lee, his critics argue, constantly badgered the secessionist government to bring troops from other areas to reinforce his army in Virginia while he consistently opposed the transfer of any of his troops to strengthen Rebel forces in the West. The result, the critics—especially Connelly—insist, was that the Confederate armies defending the western part of Rebeldom found themselves greatly outnumbered and unable to protect the crucial region entrusted to their care while Lee waged one bloody battle after another in the East and accomplished nothing except to consume Southern manpower. Lee, the critics like to quip, won victory after victory leading to defeat.

Most of Lee's detractors—with some exceptions almost as Virginia-centric as his admirers and, for that matter, many of his defenders as well (and all of them far more so than was Lee himself)—usually ignore the first allegation. Instead, they focus on the second charge that Lee was a practitioner of inappropriate offensive warfare on both the tactical and strategic levels. They point out that a revolution in military technology in the 1850s wrought a great change on the battlefields of the 1860s. The new technology involved the widespread use of rifled shoulder weapons. Those weapons used the minié ball, a conical bullet that rotated around its longitudinal axis when fired, thus giving the weapon greater range and accuracy. The metallic percussion cap, which served as a detonator when struck by the weapon's hammer, was a third important innovation. The new technology increased the maximum effective range of the standard infantry shoulder arm by a factor of five (from one hundred to five hundred yards) and made the new weapons far more reliable, especially in windy and damp weather.[12]

12. In practice, the increased effective range was usually considerably less than five times the old effective range. Terrain, wind, vegetation, and clouds of battlefield smoke would all operate to limit the effectiveness of the new weapons. Soldiers using some types of the new weapons

On the battlefield these changes greatly strengthened the tactical defense. Skilled marksmen serving as sharpshooters for the army standing on the defensive could often silence or drive away hostile artillery simply by shooting down the gunners and horses from great distances. Troops fighting on the tactical defensive could do the same to attacking enemy infantrymen as they advanced across the open ground between the opposing forces. If the defenders had time to entrench or to pile up logs, rocks, fence rails, or other objects for protection, their ability to repulse an assault increased exponentially.

It was, therefore, almost always difficult and usually very costly for a Civil War army to attack an enemy position. Victory for the army fighting on the tactical offensive was unlikely under most circumstances. Even then, battlefield triumph usually came at such a price that afterward the attacking army simply lacked the strength and found itself too disorganized by the fighting to follow up on its success. This situation was especially likely when the army making the attack was the smaller force.

For these reasons many of Lee's critics have faulted him for what they describe as his propensity for aggressive, offensive strategy and tactics. The great Rebel general, they maintain, took command of his army and rushed forth to find and attack the invaders of his beloved Virginia, constantly seeking to wage a "decisive" battle to settle the war once and for all. Some of the critics argue further that Lee followed such a course in an effort to relieve the psychological strain growing out of his own doubts about the legality and morality of secession and his own conduct in the sectional crisis of 1860–61. Lee, they assert, suffered a "cognitive disso-

---

had to estimate the distance to the target and set their sights accordingly. Such estimates had to be made hurriedly and in the heat and excitement of battle. If the soldier's estimate was off by even a few yards, the bullet would strike the ground in front of the target or soar several feet above it. In addition, some commentators have pointed out, soldiers usually had not been trained in marksmanship (as opposed to volley fire) and that factor also operated to limit the new weapons' effectiveness. Thus, the realistic increase was more like two or three times the old effective range—still enough to make Civil War battlefields far more dangerous places than were those of earlier wars. See Gerald J. Prokopowicz, "Tactical Stalemate," *North & South* 2.7 (Sept. 1999): 10–27; and the discussion by George Willard quoted in Thomas K. Tate, letter to the editor, ibid. 3.3 (Mar. 2000): 7, 94. Many units, furthermore, did not have the new weapons until well into the second year of the war and in some cases not until the third.

nance" and therefore wanted to resolve matters quickly to relieve the psychological tensions arising from his own doubts and fears about the rightness of his course of action in making war on the United States.

Such an approach naturally necessitated that he operate aggressively against the opposing army, and that aggression usually took the form of an attack, with its attendant heavy casualties, upon the enemy's position. Lee, Alan Nolan wrote, was "so committed to the offensive that he suffered grievous and irreplaceable losses that progressively limited the viability of his army." Far better, the critics argue, for Lee to have stood on the tactical defensive with, perhaps, an occasional lashing out at some isolated, vulnerable part of the Yankee force in his front.[13]

By fighting defensively, conserving his strength, and allowing the Yankees to waste their men in attacks on his fortified positions, the critics maintain, Lee would have avoided the heavy casualties that characterized his aggressive style of warfare, preserved Rebel manpower, slowly worn down the Northern will to go on with the struggle, and in so doing "won by not losing." As it was, they maintain, Lee simply achieved a series of sometimes spectacular, though meaningless, local battlefield victories at such a cost that he wound up destroying his own army. This course of action, the critics point out, resulted in 100,000 casualties in Lee's army in the first fourteen months of his command (the Seven Days through Gettysburg). The end result was total Confederate defeat. Lee's army, so the critics joke, wore itself out whipping the Yankees.

Can the western paradigm help us analyze Lee's conduct of the war and evaluate the arguments of his critics? I believe it can.

Let us begin with five general observations about Lee's detractors and their arguments. Probably the first thing that a convert to the western paradigm would notice about Lee's critics is that almost all of them are guilty to a greater or lesser degree of one of the grievous sins for which they arraign Lee. With very few exceptions these writers focus on the war in Virginia almost to the exclusion of everything that was transpiring

---

13. Nolan, *Lee Considered,* x. This view of Lee runs through Weigley, *Great Civil War.*

elsewhere. Bevin Alexander, for example, apparently writing in complete ignorance of what, in fact, happened outside Virginia, asserted, "if the Confederacy had possessed a military genius in command of its principal army [the Army of Northern Virginia], it could have been victorious irrespective of the North's material superiority." Alexander does not inform his readers how such a military genius in Virginia would have offset the loss of the West and dealt with the early 1865 appearance of Sherman's armies in northeastern North Carolina, especially if that military genius had confined his efforts to fighting on the defensive.[14]

Although most of the critics toss in an occasional sentence or two about matters beyond the boundaries of the Old Dominion, it is clear that very few of them have ever given much serious thought to any extra-Virginia events in developing their thesis. Those who harp on Lee's heavy 1862–63 losses, for example, do not seem cognizant of the fact that in the period January 1862–July 1863 inclusive, while the Rebels in Virginia lost about 110,000 men, the Confederates' western generals managed to suffer more than 100,000 casualties *and* lose the Mississippi Valley, large slices of crucial territory, several important cities, and—arguably—the war.[15]

No matter what the Rebels did in Virginia, what strategy they followed there, or what tactics Lee adopted there, they would lose the war if they lost the West unless they could find some way in the eastern theater to offset their defeats elsewhere. (The reverse is also true, but that fact is irrelevant to the present discussion.)

---

14. Alexander, *Lee's Civil War*, ix.

15. The critics who do notice the losses in the West contend that most of those casualties were prisoners who would be exchanged and go back into the Rebel army. They overlook several facts. Many exchangees came back from Northern prisoner-of-war camps or out of paroled garrisons captured after a long siege with their health so impaired that they were useless as soldiers, at least until they regained their strength and health. One of the reasons why Pemberton surrendered Vicksburg when he did was that his men were so weakened by disease and a long period of inactivity in the trenches that physically they could not have held out much longer. In any case, men who were captured were out of service for shorter or longer periods, and often their morale was wrecked by the experience of defeat, capture, and imprisonment. Finally, the critics fail to note that *somebody* had to capture Federal soldiers to exchange for the Rebels held by the Yankees. Many of the captured Confederates were swapped for unionists captured by Lee in his battles.

Lee's critics, in fact, get the whole matter backward. A locally success-ful offensive strategy in Virginia might lead to Confederate independence (depending on circumstances such as the public's perception of the course of the war). On the other hand, no defensive strategy in Virginia—no matter how successful locally—would further the Confederate quest for independence if the secessionists could not avoid defeat in the West. If Sherman's armies took Richmond from the south, it would mean the end of secession even if on the very day Sherman and his Yankees marched into the Rebel capital Lee repulsed yet another assault along the Rappa-hannock and inflicted another 25,000 casualties on the Army of the Po-tomac and did not lose a man from his own ranks in doing so.

Even when the critics do consider operations outside Virginia, they often make unrealistic assumptions about Confederate prospects in those areas and/or rely on now-outdated studies for their knowledge and in-terpretations of the happenings in those regions. Many of them, for example, assume that sending a relatively small number of reinforce-ments (say, two or three divisions) from Lee's army to the West would have enabled the western Confederates to defeat the Union armies in Tennessee, Mississippi, or Georgia. There is nothing in the records of the western Rebel generals to suggest that this would have been the case and much to indicate that it would not have been.

In this respect Lee's critics resemble a scientist who last read a pro-fessional publication in 1980 and who reaches his/her conclusions based on information in that publication and on experiments he/she conducts under ideal laboratory conditions without considering how more-recent knowledge might alter his/her intellectual framework or how such out-side factors as temperature, wind, and humidity might change the re-sults of his/her experiments. (We should note that many of these same critics lambaste Lee for his alleged ignorance of the West and of condi-tions there.)

For example, until the late 1960s, historians usually viewed Joseph E. Johnston's Atlanta campaign of 1864 as a strategic masterpiece thwarted when President Davis relieved him from command in mid-July of that year. Today most historians of the war in the West, while admitting that

Johnston's 1864 campaign in North Georgia was a brilliant military retreat, realize that it was at the same time a strategic, logistical, psychological, and political disaster of the first magnitude for the Confederates. Yet several of Lee's recent critics cite that campaign as a model of
how they think the secessionists should have carried on the war.[16]

Because they are so myopically focused on what was transpiring in
Virginia, the critics usually lose sight of the fact that military events in
the Old Dominion (like those that took place elsewhere) did not occur
in a vacuum. Battles won or lost, for example, can have a major impact
on the political, logistical, psychological, and diplomatic sides of warfare. Those facets of the struggle, in turn, often influence (and on occasion dictate) military operations. Battlefield triumphs such as Lee won
in Virginia can inspire a people to continue the great sacrifices that may
lead to eventual victory for the nation or they can influence the atti-
tudes and policies of neutral or even enemy countries.

Lee's wartime operations, in summary, should be evaluated in light of
the Confederacy's *overall* situation and the national options realistically
available to the Rebels at the time the operations were undertaken. To
judge them against some ideal, theoretical standard and to limit the evaluation to events transpiring in Virginia is, to say the least, misleading.

Readers oriented toward the western theater might also note a second characteristic exhibited by many of those who criticize Lee. Drawing comparisons with the American War for Independence and the war
in Vietnam, almost all of them assume that a protracted struggle would
have been to the advantage of the Confederacy. Such an extended conflict, they believe, would have worn down the unionists' will to go on
with the fight and Northern public opinion would have eventually forced
the Federal government to acquiesce in Southern independence.

16. See, for example, Russell Weigley, who heaps praise on Johnston for his passive campaign in Georgia during 1864 and cites it as a model for how Lee should have acted against
Grant that year. *Great Civil War,* 358–63. Yet Weigley himself writes, "a defensive strategy was
all too likely to multiply the advantages of the Union by allowing it to concentrate men and
matériel at places of its choosing and . . . consequently to stand on the defensive was even less
promising than [was] Lee's offensive strategy" (256). Though he is discussing the Gettysburg
campaign in this case, the observation applies to the 1864 campaigns as well.

In theory, of course, this assumption is valid. If the Rebels had managed to hold out until, say, 1986, most Northerners would probably have been willing to let the seceded states have their independence. Such an argument, however, ignores both the fact that the South was actually losing the war from an early date as well as the vast differences between the situation in the 1860s on the one hand and that in the 1770s or the 1960s and the 1970s on the other. "The difference between the Atlantic Ocean and Mason and Dixon's line," wrote Rossiter Johnson in 1894, was one major reason why the situation of the Confederacy was not comparable to that of the American colonists during the War for Independence.[17]

To cite but two other obvious differences, we might note that the Confederates, unlike the American colonists and the Vietnamese nationalists, had no significant assistance from other countries nor did the secessionists enjoy political leadership superior to that of their opponents. In fact, actual conditions in the 1860s almost certainly made it impossible for the Confederates to have carried on the conflict much beyond the time when they surrendered.

The longer the war continued, the longer the North had to mobilize its overwhelming resources and commit them to the conflict, while the South became weaker as its irreplaceable resources were consumed by the struggle and as the fissures in Confederate society deepened under the pressures generated by the conflict. Both Jefferson Davis and Robert E. Lee were very much aware of these facts. A cynic would also add that a prolonged conflict would only give the western Rebel generals more time to demonstrate their unfitness for command and to lose more battles, more men, more cities, and more territory.

Third, although to my knowledge none of Lee's critics has ever explicitly so stated, almost all of them, in fact, rest their arguments for an extended war on five other, less sweeping assumptions—all of them questionable at best. The critics believe that had Lee stood on the tactical defensive in Virginia, the Federal generals there would have cooperated with his strategy by hurling one massive attack after another at his fortified

17. Johnson, "Turning-Points," 42.

positions and been repulsed with heavy losses as had happened at Fredericksburg in December 1862 and at Second Cold Harbor in June 1864. Meanwhile, the critics also assume, other Confederate generals would have been able to avoid losing the war in some other area—the West, for example.[18] All the while, the critics believe, the Rebel political leadership would have proven superior to that of Abraham Lincoln in nerving the Southern people to go on with the conflict and that the Confederacy's social, political, racial, and economic institutions would have weathered the inevitable strains of such a protracted war longer than could those of the North. We might be forgiven for wondering just how long the extremely fragile institution of slavery (the Confederacy's very raison d'être) could have withstood the stresses to which an extended war and the presence of invading Union troops would have subjected it.

Included in this group of minor assumptions is a fifth that the critics apply in almost all of their comments about Lee's military operations. They assume that conditions remained static throughout the war and that, therefore, the policy that they believe would have been most conducive to Rebel military success in 1864 would also have been the best grand strategy for Lee and the secessionists to have followed in 1862 and 1863. Could it have been that the Southerners should have pursued different policies at different times, under different circumstances, and against different Yankee commanders?[19]

Fourth, many of Lee's critics usually ignore the fact that his commander in chief was Jefferson Davis, a man of some military ability, of considerable military experience, and a president who believed himself fully qualified to plan and, in general, direct the operations of his nation's armies. Davis expected to play a (if not *the*) central role in deciding the secessionists' military policies, and he usually did.

18. Nolan, who appreciates the importance of the West more than do most of Lee's critics, does admit that even if Lee had followed a defensive strategy in Virginia and if it had been "fully effective" there, the Rebels might still have lost the war elsewhere. *Lee Considered,* 67.

19. See Steven E. Woodworth, *Davis & Lee at War* (Lawrence: Univ. Press of Kansas, 1995); and Peter Carmichael, "Lee's Search for the Battle of Annihilation," *North & South* 3.5 (June 2000): 53–58.

Under the American system of government (whether Federal or Confederate), elected civilian authorities raised and controlled their nation's armed forces. Those same authorities also determined national war aims and policies and furnished supplies to the military and naval forces. Any army commander who did not cooperate with his president and with the civil authorities, did not conform to their policies, and failed to keep them advised as to what he was doing and of the situation in his front would have a very difficult task effectively commanding his army. This would be the case no matter how well the general got along with the army itself or how sound his military ideas might have been in the abstract. George B. McClellan for the North and Joseph E. Johnston for the South best exemplified this fundamental truth of Civil War command. Lee did not exercise command in a vacuum. To be effective he *had* to work with Jefferson Davis, and that was not an easy task under the best of circumstances.[20]

Finally, many writers overlook the fact that Davis's selection on June 1, 1862, of Lee to replace the wounded Joseph E. Johnston at the head of the principal Rebel army in Virginia was but one of three crucial new assignments to major commands that the secessionists made within a period of about thirty days in late May and June of that year. On May 26, a few days before Johnston fell at Seven Pines, Maj. Gen. Thomas C. Hindman received orders to take command of the demoralized Rebel forces in Arkansas.[21] On the day before Johnston fell at Seven Pines, the Confederates' main western army evacuated Corinth, Mississippi, and retreated to Tupelo, some fifty miles to the south. Gen. Pierre G. T. Beauregard, who then commanded that army, was ill. Without securing the

---

20. Some of Lee's critics have faulted him for working with his government! Fuller criticizes Lee's "subservience" to his commander in chief. *Grant and Lee*, 235, 254–55. Bevin Alexander faults Lee for following the leadership of the Confederacy's civilian authorities, "although this leadership was often militarily inept and succumbed to pressure from [local] politicians who did not want their territories occupied by Federals irrespective of the Confederacy's strategic needs." *Lost Victories*, 289. Surely the Confederacy did not need a revolt by its best general against the civilian government added to all of its other problems!

21. Hindman's assignment came from Gen. P. G. T. Beauregard, then in command of secessionist forces in the Mississippi Valley, not from Rebel authorities in Richmond.

approval of the government, he decided to take a furlough in order to recover his health. When Davis learned that Beauregard had left his post without authorization, the president removed him from command and named Gen. Braxton Bragg as his replacement. Thus, within the span of little more than a month, the Rebels found themselves with newly installed, untested commanders in all three of the war's major theaters of operations. They also found their new nation on the brink of collapse in all three areas.

The first five months of 1862 had been a time of virtually unrelieved disaster for the secessionist cause. The Federals had driven the Rebels out of Missouri and moved into Arkansas, where they were well along toward reestablishing the national authority over the northwestern quarter of that state. The Confederate government had withdrawn large numbers of troops from west of the Great River to reinforce the Rebel army in Mississippi—an action that set off panic in Arkansas and produced howls of protest and even threats of secession from the state's political leaders.

In the first five months of the year, what would become Bragg's army had been chased out of Kentucky and Tennessee and had lost some 35,000 men killed, wounded, and captured along with thousands more lost to disease. The army of which Lee assumed command on June 1 had been pushed back to the outskirts of Richmond, and its prospects for holding the Confederate capital seemed bleak at best. President Davis had sent his family off to safety in North Carolina, and administration officials were preparing for a likely order to evacuate the city.

Within a short time after they assumed command, Lee and Bragg had embarked on (separate) efforts to reverse the Rebels' gloomy situations in Virginia and in the West, and Hindman had made considerable progress in rebuilding secessionist fortunes in Arkansas. Leaving some troops in Mississippi, Bragg shifted a large part of his army eastward through Mobile, Montgomery, and Atlanta to Chattanooga—a brilliant strategic movement by railroad on a scale never attempted before. From Chattanooga he marched northward, eventually moving into Kentucky. Meanwhile, the forces he had left in Mississippi advanced into the northern portion of that state to threaten the Yankees there and in West Tennessee.

While Bragg was thus attempting to revive the secessionist cause in the West, Lee concentrated Confederate forces in Virginia, attacked the Northern army outside Richmond, and drove it away. Lee then moved northward, defeated another Yankee army at Manassas, and chased it into the Washington fortifications, thereby shifting the war in the East from the outskirts of Richmond to the outskirts of Washington. Early in September he crossed the Potomac into Maryland. While Bragg and Lee were striking northward, Hindman ruthlessly conscripted men and impressed matériel to rebuild secessionist strength in Arkansas.

By mid-October this "high tide" of the Confederacy had crested and begun to ebb. Lee had encountered the Union army along Antietam Creek in western Maryland on September 17. Although the Rebels had repulsed every Yankee attack that day, they took staggering losses that so weakened their army that Lee withdrew to Virginia during the night of September 18–19. Early in October secessionist armies in northern Mississippi suffered defeats in battles with Yankee forces at Iuka and Corinth. A few days later in Kentucky, Bragg fought the Battle of Perryville in which his outnumbered troops managed to win a limited tactical victory but were forced to abandon their campaign and withdraw to Middle Tennessee. Hindman's harsh measures had long since stirred up so many complaints in Arkansas that in July Davis had placed him under command of the ineffective Maj. Gen. Theophilus H. Holmes.

The Rebels fought three more large battles before 1862 came to its end. On December 7 at Prairie Grove in Arkansas they suffered a major defeat. Six days later Lee won an easy triumph against the Yankees at Fredericksburg, and over New Year's, Bragg lost the Battle of Stones River in Middle Tennessee.

The last seven months of 1862 thus saw nine major military engagements: four under Lee in the East (the Seven Days, Second Manassas, Antietam, and Fredericksburg); four in the West (Iuka, Corinth, Perryville, and Stones River); and Prairie Grove in the Trans-Mississippi. Lee fought the last three of his campaigns on the tactical defensive (although his army did deliver a devastating counterattack at Second Manassas). The western Confederates fought *all four* of their major actions on the tactical offensive. At Prairie Grove the Rebels first assumed the offensive and then switched to a defensive posture, a serious mistake because in so doing they simply stood by while the Yankees united their previously separated forces.

These campaigns all took place during a period when the Confederacy enjoyed its greatest strength relative to the North and when it appeared that the Confederates might be able to win one or more great military victories that would compel the Federal government to recognize Southern independence.[22] Under such circumstances it seemed appropriate that the Rebel armies take the initiative and operate offensively on the strategic, if not the tactical, level. Yet during that time Lee fought three of his four major engagements on the tactical defensive. The western secessionist generals, however, fought on the tactical offensive in all four of their major battles. In light of these facts, what are we to make of the accusation that Lee was too wedded to the tactical offensive?

During the fall of 1862, in the aftermath of the great Confederate offensive effort, it became clear to any reasonably competent observer that extremely serious command and personnel problems had surfaced in the Rebels' main western army. Almost as soon as Bragg began his withdrawal from Kentucky, bitter criticism of him and his management of the campaign broke out in the army, the press, and in the Congress.

Maj. Gen. Edmund Kirby Smith, one of Bragg's chief subordinates, sent his medical director to Richmond with a letter to the president. In this document, now lost, Smith expressed severe criticism of Bragg. Meanwhile, Leonidas Polk and William J. Hardee, Bragg's other two top subordinates, launched their ruthless campaign to undermine Bragg's influence in his own army and in public opinion in order to bring about his removal from command. Their efforts, exacerbated by Bragg's own

22. Harsh, *Confederate Tide Rising*, 12–13.

wretched personality, soon led to an internecine struggle within the army that was to divide the officers into pro-Bragg and anti-Bragg factions and continue in one form or another almost until the end of the war. It greatly weakened the Confederate effort in the West and thus the Rebels' overall military prospects.

So loud and so rapidly did the clamor grow that in late October Davis summoned Bragg to Richmond to explain his conduct. After talking with the general, the president then separately called Bragg's three chief subordinates to the capital. Two of them—Polk and Smith—went. Hardee sent word that he could add nothing to what Polk and Smith had to say.[23]

As the uproar continued in the West, President Davis attempted to bolster the Rebels' prospects there. First, he assigned Gen. Joseph E. Johnston, who had finally recovered from his Seven Pines wound, to overall command of Confederate forces in Tennessee and Mississippi. Second, in December the president left Richmond to pay a personal visit to the western army, then encamped near Murfreesboro, Tennessee.

Neither of these steps produced much good, and as the winter wore on the clamor in the western army continued and grew worse. All concerned bore some part of the blame for the problem, but the key to its bitterness and continuation was Davis's flat refusal to face up to and deal with the problem of Polk—that is, to make a choice between Bragg and Polk. Conditions became even worse once Davis and Johnston allowed the ill feeling and distrust that had long existed between them to resurface and intensify. Meanwhile, the Federals built up their strength in the region and began their probes at Vicksburg.

In the situation that existed in and after the early winter of 1862–63, any reasonably keen observer of Confederate political and military affairs could have foreseen that the Rebels were heading for more major military disasters in Tennessee and/or Mississippi unless they resolved the personnel and command problems that so hampered them in those areas.

23. On the sorry command situation in the Rebels' main western army, see Connelly, *Army of the Heartland;* and *Autumn of Glory: The Army of Tennessee, 1862–1865* (Baton Rouge: Louisiana State Univ. Press, 1971).

Only Jefferson Davis could take corrective action, and he either could not bring himself to do so or he simply did not understand the problem and assumed, as he often did, that all of his generals were men of competence and good will who were totally devoted to the welfare of the Confederacy and who would cooperate for the benefit of the cause no matter how much they hated, despised, loathed, and distrusted him or each other.

It was against this background that a great debate about Confederate grand strategy broke out among Rebel leaders in the spring of 1863. As the Federals closed on and then laid siege to Vicksburg and Port Hudson, proposals surfaced to take troops from Lee's army and send them to reinforce the Southerners in Mississippi in an effort to save Vicksburg. This strategy was largely the work of Secretary of War James A. Seddon. A variation of this plan, put forth by the western concentration bloc, called for reinforcements from Lee's army to go to Tennessee and to strengthen Bragg's army for an offensive there that might induce the Northern government to shift its forces away from Vicksburg to protect Kentucky, Ohio, and Indiana.

Meanwhile, President Davis held for a time to his longstanding belief that the secessionists could shuttle troops back and forth between Tennessee and Mississippi to concentrate and defeat the enemy first in one place and then in the other. Joseph E. Johnston, overall commander of Rebel forces in those states, on whom the responsibility for executing Davis's plan would fall, maintained that such a scheme could not possibly work. He countered the president's suggestions with the argument that the distances the troops would have to travel under Davis's proposal were too great for the plan to be effective. Far better, he opined, to order troops from west of the Mississippi to cross the Great River to help defend Vicksburg. Naturally, Johnston's proposal met with strong disapproval from the Confederate commander in the Trans-Mississippi, who argued that such a transfer of troops from his command was not practicable. (We should note that all the evidence indicates that had the Confederates undertaken such a movement, the Trans-Mississippi troops would have deserted en masse and all of Arkansas would have been opened to conquest by the Yankees.)

We do not know how closely Lee followed the situation in the Confederate high command that winter and spring. He was by nature a very private, reticent man who tended to play things close to his vest—a wise precaution for a general in any situation, especially his, even if it frustrates historians—and he usually had the good sense not to reveal very much about himself. For this reason we have to try to discern Lee's ideas on grand strategy from occasional remarks here and there in his correspondence and recorded conversations and, above all, from his actions.

Lee was certainly well aware of the major military developments in the West, and it seems most unlikely that he would have remained ignorant of at least the general thrusts of the criticisms directed at Bragg, especially once the attacks on that officer had gotten into the newspapers. In early 1862, when he had worked in Richmond as Jefferson Davis's military adviser, Lee had had the opportunity to observe the deteriorating relationship between the president and Joseph E. Johnston that became obvious during those months and that had so hampered Rebel military operations in Virginia at the time.

It would, therefore, have been natural for Lee to have concluded sometime in the winter of 1862–63 or perhaps in the following spring that the Rebels' plight in the West would only get worse and that the Confederacy would lose the war unless its armies could win a quick victory that would compel the Federal government to recognize Southern independence. Any intelligent observer could see that Lee's army was the only Rebel force likely to gain such a success.

That winter too Lee suffered the first of the heart problems (perhaps angina pectoris) that were to plague him off and on for the remainder of his life. His health thus may have added a degree of urgency to his ideas about Rebel grand strategy. Should his condition recur or worsen and he die before the war was won, the Confederacy had no one to take his place and would have no realistic hope of gaining its independence. The fact that Lee's army operated near Washington and the importance that the Northern government and public always attached to events in the eastern theater meant that any success Lee's army could win there—especially should that success come on Northern soil—would have a much greater effect on public opinion and morale and probably on the policy of the Federal government than would any victories the Confederates might win elsewhere.

Thus, when Richmond authorities queried Lee about sending a division or two from the Army of Northern Virginia to the West, Lee responded with arguments as to why such a strategy would be unlikely to achieve success. He opposed the transfer of any of his soldiers to the West because he faced a massive Yankee army in Virginia and because the Confederates could not "change troops from one department to another" as rapidly as the Federals could. He also feared the unhealthful climate in the lower Mississippi Valley, which he thought would force the enemy to retire as summer approached and also would decimate the ranks of any unacclimated Confederate troops sent there from Virginia. Finally, he mentioned what he called "the uncertainty of . . . [the] application" of troops sent to Mississippi or Tennessee. By this last he seems tactfully to have been expressing his doubts as to the competence of Confederate generals in the West.[24]

Instead of rushing troops back and forth across the countryside to meet Federal threats after they materialized, Lee proposed another strategy. He would have Confederate forces in unthreatened areas assume what he called "the aggressive" and in so doing disrupt Federal plans and force the unionists to abandon their own offensive efforts in order to defend what they already held, if not their home territory. It was this line of thinking that led Lee to propose what became the Gettysburg campaign.

The Pennsylvania proposal was Lee's most controversial wartime recommendation. If my suggestion is valid, the proposal owed at least a

---

24. Lee, *The Wartime Papers of Robert E. Lee,* eds. Clifford Dowdey and Louis H. Manarin (Boston: Little, Brown, 1961), 430, 433–34, 482. One should note that virtually all of the evidence cited by Lee's critics to demonstrate his devotion to aggressive warfare dates from the winter of 1862–63 or later. See, for example, Nolan, *Lee Considered,* 73–77.

part of its origin to Lee's realization of the dire straits the Rebels faced in the West; to his (well-founded) assumption that any efforts they attempted there were likely to fail; to the realization that time was not on the Rebels' side, both because it gave the North the opportunity to marshal its great resources and also because the South was already losing the war in the West; and, perhaps, to an awareness of his own mortality and the consequent realization that if he was to win independence for the South, he had better do so quickly.

For what it may be worth, I think that Lee's analysis of the Confederacy's overall military situation was correct. In the late part of 1862 and the early months of 1863, it became increasingly obvious that unless Lee could win a great victory in the East, the secessionists would suffer eventual defeat in the West. In effect, the situation had become one in which the Federals would win the war in the West if they did not lose it in the East—the Yankee version of "winning by not losing." As historian Steven Woodworth has commented, using a boxing analogy, Lee proposed that the secessionists try to win by a knockout in the East before they lost on points in the West.[25]

In 1864 the situation changed again. The basic outlines of the war's military history remained fixed—Union victory in the West; bloody stalemate in the East. Two new factors, however, revived the Rebels' hopes that year. The approaching presidential election in the North offered the possibility that, if Northern voters perceived the war as going badly for the Union cause, they might sweep the Lincoln administration out of office and replace it by a new government that would be willing to accept Confederate independence.

Grant's arrival in Virginia also worked in the Southerners' favor, although that fact did not become visible for some time. His willingness to attack Lee allowed the great Confederate leader to fight on the tactical defensive for most of the spring and summer, resulting in horrific casualties among the Yankees that appalled Northerners without producing

25. McMurry, "Pennsylvania Gambit"; Woodworth, conversations with author.

any offsetting victories. Even Lee's harshest critics praise his defensive fighting in the 1864 Overland campaign against Grant.

Once again, however, whatever chance the Confederates had was lost when the western Rebel generals proved unable to block Sherman's invasion of Georgia or even to inflict heavy casualties on the Union armies there. Sherman's success gave Lincoln the great victory he needed to assure his reelection. That triumph at the polls meant that the Federal government would see the war through to final and complete victory.

The most telling argument in favor of Lee's concept of how the Confederates should have carried on the war and his conduct of military operations in the East is the sorry record of the Rebel commanders in the West. Lee may not have seen the Confederacy's predicament with absolute clarity, but his actions and an occasional sentence or two here and there in his correspondence are strong indications that he had developed at least a basic understanding of the fact that, by New Year's Day, 1863, the secessionists' most realistic—if not their only—hope was that he could win a victory in the East that would bring independence to the South. Otherwise, the best the Rebels could hope for was to maintain a stalemate in Virginia while their position in the West continued to erode and they eventually lost the war. Should Lee's health problems prove very serious, the secessionists almost certainly could not even maintain a stalemate in Virginia for very long.

Lee understood, or sensed, or was driven by psychological disorders to, or had the blind luck to stumble on (your choice—it really does not matter) the great strategic truth of Confederate military history: Unless he could win the war in the East, the South inevitably would lose it in the West. The constant failures in the West and the possibility that his own health would deteriorate meant that he had to win his war quickly. The Rebels' overall military situation, in effect, demanded an aggressive war on his part. Whatever the reason that led him to the conclusions he reached and whether or not he fully understood the situation, Robert E. Lee saw the Rebels' overall military predicament far better than did any of his Confederate contemporaries and much better than have all of his modern critics.

PART SEVEN

Conclusions

P erhaps the best way to evaluate both Confederate grand strategy in general and Robert E. Lee's strategic concepts in particular is to think of the problem in terms of the three possible forms the war could have taken relative to the length of the conflict. The war could have been short, say no longer than a year or two; it could have been of intermediate length, two to seven years; or it could have been a long struggle lasting more than seven years.

We can visualize how, theoretically, the Confederacy could have prevailed in a short war had the secessionists been able to organize quickly and to take the offensive before the North could mobilize its men and resources for the conflict. Of course, the Confederates actually could have done no such thing. Not even half of the slave states seceded prior to the firing on Fort Sumter, and those remaining loyal until the war's outbreak included three of what were to be the Confederacy's four most important states—North Carolina, Tennessee, and Virginia. Georgia was the other state with an economy and a population base that made her essential to the Rebels. Three other important slave states, Maryland, Missouri, and Kentucky, did not secede at all. (As pointed out above, however, the last two each had a rump Confederate government and representation in the Confederate Congress, and citizens of all three formed organized military units in Rebel service.)

By the time the Southerners could have gotten their new government organized and raised, trained, equipped, and deployed an army, the Federal forces would have been strong enough to thwart such an offensive. The short-war scenario for a Rebel victory is only theoretical. It is also irrelevant to an evaluation of Lee's generalship both because the Old Dominion and hence Lee did not join the first wave of secession and because whatever opportunity for such a short struggle that might once have existed had passed long before Lee played any significant role in the development of Confederate grand strategy or assumed command of a major Confederate field force. We should also note that such a war would have necessitated that the secessionists act completely on the offensive.[1]

As mentioned in Part 6 above, many commentators on the war have assumed that the Confederates could have achieved their independence by holding out until the Northern public lost the will to continue the conflict. In theory such a course would have brought Confederate independence *if the Rebels could have made it through the intermediate war years without losing the struggle, and if in the meantime they could have preserved their social, economic, political, and—above all— racial institutions.* It seems evident that it would have been impossible for them to have accomplished either of these feats, given what happened in the West during the first two years of the war.

By June 1, 1862, when Lee took command in Virginia, the Yankees had already dealt secession a series of serious—arguably mortal—blows along the western rivers. Over the next twelve months Rebel fortunes in the West continued to slide downhill, and it became less and less likely that the Confederates could avoid defeat "by not losing" since they were, in fact, losing. They simply could not make it through the intermediate stage of the war to get to the long-term conflict. One way or another, the fate of the Southern Confederacy would be settled in the intermediate stage.

Faced with this reality, Lee seems to have realized sometime in the winter of 1862–63 that the Confederacy would inevitably lose the war unless it could win it. Therefore, the Rebels' best—almost certainly their only—chance to gain independence by such a grand strategy was for him to inflict a great defeat on the Union army in the East before the secessionist generals in the West lost the war there. In truth, Lee's prescription for winning Confederate independence accorded far better with the actual overall conditions then facing the Rebels than did any of the proposals made by other secessionists at the time or those since put forth by the general's critics. In large part the critics' misunderstanding of the predicament of the Confederacy and of Lee's remedy arises from

1. Bevin Alexander faults Jefferson Davis for not having Rebel forces invade Maryland in July 1861 after the First Battle of Manassas. *Lost Victories,* 32–35.

their common failure (and often refusal) to view the war as a whole. Their usual myopic focus on the conflict in Virginia has led them astray.

Although Lee seems correctly to have diagnosed the Confederacy's plight and to have prescribed the only cure that offered any possibility to save the patient, he was never able to implement it completely or successfully. To a great extent Lee's failure in the former endeavor stemmed from the fact that he never managed to get President Davis to commit himself wholeheartedly to his analysis of the secessionists' predicament and his strategy to deal with it. Lee always had to be very careful in his relations with the president, who was extremely reluctant to share his constitutional authority as commander in chief of Confederate military forces with anyone. The general accordingly had sometimes to work around Davis, to flatter him, and on occasion to nudge the president with subtle suggestions and hints.[2]

Despite his best efforts, Lee often failed to move the chief executive to commit the Confederate government completely to what Lee saw as the secessionists' best course of action. Although Davis agreed in principle with Lee's emphasis on the need for the Rebels to seize the initiative and to wage an aggressive war (what the present generation would call a "proactive" war), the president proved too cautious to make an all-out effort and unable to realize that under the circumstances facing the Confederacy—constant failure in the West—any other course was certain to lead to overall national defeat.[3]

---

2. Some critics have faulted Lee for what they regard as the obsequious way in which he dealt with Davis—a practice technically known as "sucking up." As historian William C. Davis has pointed out, however, there are two kinds of "sucking up" to those in authority. One type is practiced by basically worthless people who seek to win favor and promotion by flattering their superiors; the second is often necessary to move the boss to get out of the way and let you do your job. Since Lee already held the highest grade in the Confederate army, he clearly belongs in the latter category. Davis, conversations with author.

3. "Should the opportunity occur for striking the enemy a successful blow do not let it escape you," Lee wrote to "Stonewall" Jackson on June 8, 1862. Lee, *Papers,* 187. For other examples of Lee's emphasis on the Rebels' need to conduct proactive operations, see his spring 1862 correspondence in ibid., 155–75. Such an aggressive war, however, did not necessarily mean taking the tactical offensive. See also the comments in Harsh, *Confederate Tide Rising,* 18–26.

In effect, Lee had to deal with three opposing forces during the war. The Yankee army in his front was the obvious opponent. The second was the western concentration bloc, which sought to divert Rebel resources to areas where, Lee realized, they were less likely (or even unlikely) to be used wisely or effectively. The third was President Davis's unwillingness (for whatever reason) to decide to commit his government wholeheartedly to *any* course of action.

Often such strategic decisions would have to be made quickly in order to take advantage of whatever opportunity the very fluid military situation then offered. To delay was almost certainly to lose all chance of success. Davis did not like to make decisions, and he especially did not like to make them quickly. The Confederate chief executive, wrote Sir Frederick Maurice, "could never make up his mind to take risks for a great end."[4] Given the Rebels' constantly deteriorating fortunes in the West, the Confederates had to take risks somewhere. Not to do so was simply to sit back and await inevitable defeat. Would the Southerners have been better off to entrust such risky operations to Lee or to one of the western generals?

The best example of this problem arose during the early summer of 1863 when Davis sent some reinforcements to Lee for the Gettysburg campaign, but he overruled his general about others either withheld to guard various points or sent to Mississippi in what proved to be a vain effort to organize an army to relieve Vicksburg. The president would not use those men to create, as Lee urged him to do, another force in Virginia that could maneuver so as to threaten Washington and thereby compel the Federals to protect that city as well as to pursue Lee's army off to the northwest.

Davis exhibited the politician's common tendency to try to do too many things in an effort to satisfy too many competing interests at once and to split the difference between opposing viewpoints, thereby guaranteeing that none of his efforts would be strong enough to succeed.

4. Quoted in Henry Steele Commager, ed., *The Defeat of the Confederacy: A Documentary Survey* (Princeton, N.J.: D. Van Nostrand, 1964), 45–46.

He would allow Lee to attempt his daring campaign beyond the Potomac and give him some reinforcements to do so, but he would not strengthen him as much as possible in an all-out effort to win a great victory on Northern soil. In this regard he put the Confederacy in the position of the ox hung up on the fence, unable (that is, not strong enough) to gore one way or to kick the other (to borrow and paraphrase Lincoln's famous analogy).

Lee, of course, also failed in his effort to win the great victory. In large part his failures can be explained by his own mistakes and those of many of his subordinate generals. In large part too they stemmed from the prowess of the Yankee troops whom he faced at Gettysburg and in other battles.

Would the Rebels have won if their president had made a complete commitment to Lee's grand strategy in 1863? Would that strategy have succeeded had the chief executive done so? We can never know. Would the Rebels have lost the war by losing in the West if they did not follow something close to the strategy that Lee advocated in the East? Beyond any rational doubt they would have—and in fact they did.

The defeats of 1863 (Gettysburg, Vicksburg, Chattanooga) left the Rebels far too weak to undertake further major offensive efforts. The changed conditions of 1864, however, gave them a chance to apply their version of "winning by not losing," and Lee waged a brilliant defensive war in Virginia that summer, holding Richmond and inflicting horrific losses on the Union army in the Old Dominion—losses that came close to demoralizing the North. The Rebels in the West, however, never managed to overcome their many problems, and once again, defeats in the West nullified Lee's success in the East.

And so the Confederacy went down to defeat, though not because of Robert E. Lee. The victories Lee won in Virginia—and only those victories—kept the Southern nation alive for two or three years beyond the time when it otherwise would have expired. They also nerved soldiers and (white) civilians alike all across the Confederacy, inspiring them to go on in the face of almost constant failures on other fronts. If one wishes to know how and why the Confederacy held out for so long in the face of such great odds, he or she should look to Virginia in general and to General Lee in particular. If, however, one wishes to know how and why the Confederacy failed, he or she must look elsewhere.

Defeat for the Rebels came in the West. Although the geography and other factors of that region conspired against the Southerners, their failure there stemmed more than anything else directly from the conduct (or misconduct) of a number of their high-ranking generals—especially from that of Leonidas Polk. Ultimate responsibility for the debacle that was the story of the Confederate war effort in the West, however, is to be found at an even higher level.

Jefferson Davis appointed the generals who served in the West; he assigned those men to the posts they held, often kept them in command long after they had demonstrated their unsuitability for positions of such great responsibility, and on several occasions interfered with their plans by issuing instructions directly to their subordinates. Except for brief periods now and then, Davis simply could not bring himself to focus on the obvious problem that was the western high command or to take the action that would give his army commanders in the West a better chance to gain success, postpone defeat, or at least avoid disaster.

Davis also made a number of serious policy errors in dealing with the West and usually would not change his practices until after some great disaster compelled him to do so. With the exception of a few months at several times during the war, for example, he would not give any commander authority over all Rebel forces in the West. In the fall of 1862 he even refused to give Bragg control of all the Confederate troops operating in east-central Kentucky, preferring instead to have three independent Rebel commands there, each pursuing its commanding general's own plans and no one in overall charge of their efforts. Davis, we should note, assumed that the three commanders would cooperate for the good of the cause. The president could not plead ignorance in this matter. He was well aware of the dangers inherent in divided command.[5]

---

5. If individual Rebel commanders in Mississippi "each act[s] for himself," Davis wrote to Bragg on September 19, 1862, "disaster to all must be the probable result." *OR,* vol. 17, 2:707.

The president often neglected the West and focused on the minutiae of the war in Virginia. Most serious of all he refused, until it was too late (October 1863), to make a clear choice between Braxton Bragg and Leonidas Polk, even when it became obvious that the latter's bad conduct was greatly hampering the military efforts of the former and that the bad feelings between the two generals were taking the Confederacy straight down the road to eventual defeat.

Jefferson Davis, mostly by acts of omission, and Leonidas Polk, by acts of commission—not Robert E. Lee—played the key roles in bringing about defeat in a war that the Confederates otherwise had a very good chance of winning.

Index

Note: The counterfactual parts (Parts 1, 2, and 3) of the essay are not indexed.